A Reading of
MOBY-DICK

A Reading of
MOBY-DICK

By M.O. PERCIVAL

1967

OCTAGON BOOKS, INC.

New York

Reprinted 1967
by special arrangement with The University of Chicago Press

OCTAGON BOOKS, INC.
175 FIFTH AVENUE
NEW YORK, N. Y. 10010

LIBRARY OF CONGRESS CATALOG CARD NUMBER: 67-18779

Printed in U.S.A. by
NOBLE OFFSET PRINTERS, INC.
NEW YORK 3, N. Y.

TO

ELEANOR

Who Set It Going

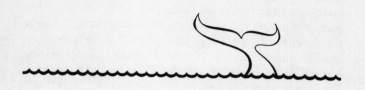

CALL ME ISHMAEL." Has any story a better beginning? We know that our guide, philosopher, and friend is of a tribe that thinks its own thoughts and goes its own ways; we know that his ways will take him to the wilderness—a wilderness of waters, it soon turns out to be; we may even suspect that if he encounters dire peril he will be miraculously rescued. The purpose of his intended journey, we are told, is peace of mind. Always and everywhere, the opening chapter goes on to say, the troubled heart has sought tranquillity beside still or running waters. About the time that Ishmael may be supposed to have betaken himself quietly to ship, Henry Thoreau quietly betook himself to the banks of Walden Pond in order to drive life into a corner and make it deliver up its secret. But Ishmael's problems were not scaled to the dimensions of Walden Pond. He needed to know the worst—the horrors of the deep—in order that he might, if possible, "come to friendly terms with all the inmates of the place one lodges in." But what of that most terrifying inmate, the Leviathan? Can a covenant be made with him? As the monsters of the deep swam into Ishmael's imagination, they culminated in "endless processions of the whale, and, mid most of them all, one grand hooded phantom, like a snow hill in the air." This is Moby Dick, the symbol of the evil that frets and baffles men in their pursuit of good. For Ishmael, as for Ahab, the pursuit of the whale is a study in good and evil.

It may seem needless to restate what the book states so clearly, but the basic theme can hardly be omitted. Nor can another theme be overlooked—the theme of Fate. Ishmael well knows, when he thinks deeply, that his journey seaward, however much it answers to his spiritual need and his intellectual curiosity, is not entirely of his own devising. No, the stage was set and the play conceived and dated for production "a long time ago," and "a long time ago" may well mean, in this context, "before the foundations of the world." As succeeding chapters make their report and the forces of the narrative begin to gather, we become aware that

we are on the eve of both a fated and a fateful journey—
one from which the travelers will not return.

Before the ship gets under way there is a convergence
of personalities and purposes which begin to weave the
allegory. Like a certain other traveler setting out to
explore the heart of darkness, Ishmael encounters signs
and portents which betoken tragic consequences. His
New Bedford night was spent at the Spouter Inn, in
whose wide, low, straggling entry there hung a dimly
terrifying painting—the heart of darkness itself—out of
which, attentively observed, emerged a faint resem-
blance to the great Leviathan. As you entered the dark-
looking den which was the bar, you seemed to be en-
tering a whale's head, while behind the bar stood Jonah
(so they called him) dispensing deliriums and death.
A warning, surely; and one that Ishmael might have
recalled when he saw Captain Ahab take his stand upon
the deck (or behind the bar) of the "Pequod"—a ship
decked out to resemble a whale's head—and dispense to
the beguiled and deluded crew a drink which was the
vehicle of delirium and death.

The next day, which happened to be a Sunday, there
came another warning, when Ishmael listened to a
sermon preached by the famous Father Mapple to a
congregation of sailors and sailors' wives and widows.
Ominous that Jonah should provide the text. The story
is not so much recounted as re-enacted—re-enacted and
moralized with the vividness and passion of a Negro
spiritual. But the sermon is not a wayward chapter.
The story of Jonah has a bearing upon Ahab's story.
It might have stood as epilogue. Instead, it stands as
a kind of prologue, a rule of right by which to deter-

mine the nature and extent of Ahab's wrong. The rule of right is simply this: Obedience to the will of God; self-surrender, not self-affirmation. "And if we obey God," Father Mapple says, "we must disobey ourselves; and it is in this disobeying ourselves, wherein the hardness of obeying God consists." Jonah willed obedience to self and became a prisoner in the belly of a whale.

> "The ribs and terrors in the whale,
> Arched over me a dismal gloom,
> While all God's sun-lit waves rolled by,
> And lift me deepening down to doom.
>
> "I saw the opening maw of hell,
> With endless pains and sorrows there;
> Which none but they that feel can tell—
> Oh, I was plunging to despair."

The analogy is clear. Self-willed as Jonah, self-willed, one might add, as Timon, Ahab turned his solitary cabin into a cave of hate, like Timon; into a maw of hell, like Jonah; and drove his ship and crew from sunlit waters into dark seas and howling gales—even into such a whale-dominated chaos as Ishmael had contemplated in the picture in the Spouter Inn. But no penitent cry to God ever came from the heart of Ahab. He embraced his fate proudly, in the belief that he had been cast for such a part by those stage-managers, the Fates, long ago.

Another sermon might have been preached to illuminate Ahab's character and fate, but it is suggested merely. It would have been based upon the story of King Ahab in the Book of Kings. He it was who married a foreign princess (Jezebel) and was persuaded by her to introduce the worship of Baal, her people's god. In permitting this new cult to be established, King Ahab "forsook the commandments of the Lord," like Jonah. There were now two gods in Israel, Jehovah and Baal, one true, one false; one ethical, one unethical; one whose principle was spirit, one whose principle was nature. For this Baal was a sun-god, but the god of a natural, not a spiritual, sun—a sun, it might be said, whose light was darkness. He was one of those apostate angels (Milton says) who

> durst fix
> Their Seats long after next the Seat of God,
> Their Altars by his Altar, Gods ador'd
> Among the Nations round, and durst abide
> *Jehovah* thundring out of *Sion*, thron'd
> Between the Cherubim; yea, often plac'd
> Within his Sanctuary it self their Shrines,
> Abominations; and with cursed things
> His holy Rites, and solemn Feasts profan'd,
> And with their darkness durst affront his light.

In contrast with Milton's eloquence, how simple and vivid and realistic Father Mapple could have made the story. The king, the critical moment, the ambitious marriage, the fatal step, the rival gods, the triumph of Elijah, the death of the wicked king in battle, the dogs licking up his blood, and, to point a moral, the justice of such a fate upon a king who went a whoring after false gods. The analogy suggested by Ahab's name must not be pressed too far, but it cannot be ignored. Captain Ahab, like King Ahab, forsook the commandments of the Lord. He knew that vengeance was God's prerogative, not man's. He knew that the god of the natural man must be superseded by the god of the spiritual man, whose qualities are love and mercy and forgiveness. These things he knew as one knows principles not yet challenged in a crisis. But, brooding first over his own wrong and then over the wrongs of the whole world, he came to doubt that the God of love and mercy and forgiveness, or even the God of righteousness, was the living God. At best, there must be another God, embodying the principle of evil. Thus there came to be two gods in Captain Ahab's mind, as there were in King Ahab's country. Long and passionate contemplation of the duality of good and evil caused him finally to cleave to evil rather than to good, so that he became an evil thing himself, an apostate, a blasphemer, a child of darkness. In the end he was slain in battle, and the sharks (presumably) licked up his blood.

The biblical analogy would lead us to expect a character named Elijah. Such a one there is, but he has little in common except the name with the mighty prophet who challenged King Ahab and met and mastered the priests of Baal. Yet this half-witted namesake of Elijah really has the gift. He knows Ahab's past and future; and what he tells with "insane earnestness" is enough to deter a hardier soul than Ishmael; but prophets, even when they speak with solemn, instead of insane, earnestness are seldom listened to in time. Elijah's earnestness is tempered by the admission that "what's signed, is signed; and what's to be, will be; and then again, perhaps it wont be, after all. Anyhow, it's all fixed and arranged a'ready; and some sailors or other must go with him, I suppose; as well these as any other men, God pity 'em! Morning to ye, shipmates, morning; the ineffable heavens bless ye; I'm sorry I stopped ye." Possibly thinking that "perhaps it wont be, after all," Elijah dogged their footsteps; but his first supposition was the right one. What's signed is signed, especially if the papers were drawn up "a long time ago."

The crew assemble, the ship is ready. On a Christmas Day, toward nightfall, the "Pequod," fiercely named and fiercely manned, and so fiercely tricked out and garnished with trophies of her enemy the whale that she seemed a very "cannibal of a craft"—on Christmas Day, the day of good will to men, the "Pequod" sailed out into the dark in pursuit of vengeance.

II

For several days after the ship sailed, Captain Ahab remained within his cabin, delaying there not with a view to making a dramatic entrance but wrestling with an evil and unclean spirit. At last the struggle was won (or lost), the decision made, and Captain Ahab took his stand upon the quarter-deck. A single glance at his face revealed the iron will behind it, but it revealed something more—something mysterious and sinister, a suffering that was nothing less than "a crucifixion." What good spirit is being crucified is not at first apparent; the suffering alone is visible and clear. It is manifest in his figure, which is not only hard and spare but that of a man "cut away from the stake"; it is manifest in his brow, where furrows have been eaten by the burning fire shut up in his bones. One thinks of another and greater rebel (Satan), upon whose face

Deep scars of Thunder had intrencht, and care
Sat on his faded cheek, but under Browes
Of dauntless courage, and considerate Pride
Waiting revenge.

When the hidden fire is at last identified, it is just this:
considerate pride waiting revenge. And could the
hidden thoughts which lighted the fire be read, they
would be as Samson's:

. . . restless thoughts, that like a deadly swarm
Of Hornets arm'd, no sooner found alone,
But rush upon me thronging, and present
Times past, what once I was, and what am now.

What once I was: a proud and courageous whaling
captain, sound in every limb. What I am now: a humil-
iated cripple, "dismasted" of one leg by a whale.

As the days pass, it becomes increasingly evident
that the fire in Ahab's bones is growing in intensity.
We are not told what fueled the flames, but we can
easily imagine. A sense of intolerable wrong; the will
to be avenged; the clear understanding by one part of
his mind that what the other part plans is mad; the
feeling, nevertheless, that some mysterious force is
pushing him on irresistibly and that, anyway, there is
grandeur in such madness—a whirl of thoughts like
these breaks out in relentless pacing of the deck, in a
vehement temper, in sleepless nights. The very feasibil-
ity of the plan, to say nothing of its morality, tormented
him. For it was nothing less than to possess the minds
of the entire crew and enlist their energies along with
his in the pursuit of a mysterious white whale called
"Moby Dick," the very one that had bitten off his leg.
But how impose his will upon the rest? Not by force,

certainly; rather by Satan's way: "Not force, but well coucht fraud, well woven snares." As the decisive hour approached, the lines in his brow went deeper, his body seemed all mind and will. At last, the fraud being formulated, the snares well woven, Captain Ahab ordered the crew upon the quarter-deck.

It drew near to the close of day. Suddenly he came to a halt by the bulwarks, and inserting his bone leg into the auger-hole there, and with one hand grasping a shroud, he ordered Starbuck to send everybody aft.

"Sir!" said the mate, astonished at an order seldom or never given on ship-board except in some extraordinary case.

"Send everybody aft," repeated Ahab. "Mast-heads, there! come down!"

Even then, with the crew assembled and waiting anxiously to hear, Captain Ahab faltered. A protest came from within—the voice of conscience. Never to be stilled for good, it had to be stilled now, else he would lose ignominiously, by default. And so the pacing of the deck began again, Ahab unmindful of the wondering crew, concerned alone with the pangs of conscience. But the insurgency of conscience was short-lived. Passion soon prevailed, first upon Ahab, then upon his men, whom he was presently exhorting with such force and guile that he drew them, as by enchantment, into his own orbit. He leagued them together in a mighty oath to chase down a certain white-headed whale—"the same that some call Moby Dick."

The crew splice hands upon it; but promises made in heat may be made more firm and lasting if tempered in magic potion and solemn ceremony. Captain Ahab gathers the crew around him circle-wise, the three mates with their lances at his side, the harpooners in front of him, their irons in hand. One by one they yield their will to his; eye meets eye, and the master-eye prevails. Having subdued them to the mood of communicants, Ahab starts the cup around. The ceremony is said to be a revival, "in some sort," of an ancient custom; but it is more than that. It is a diabolical communion, though the crew does not fully realize it; it is even more, for there are, by design or chance, some overtones from the Black Mass. Of this particular form of Satanism, the ritual is said to include black candles and black blood, the cross upside down, prayers and ceremonies backward, invocation of the devil, and ceremonies at night with poisonous brews and oaths of sin and hate. The drink that goes around is simply sailors' grog, but it seems to be transformed into something insidious. "Short draughts—long swallows, men; 'tis hot as Satan's hoof. So, so; it goes round excellently. It spiralizes in ye; forks out at the serpent-snapping eye." The crew having drunk, the three mates lay their lances crosswise before their captain, while he grasps them at the center, gazing, the while, intently at the mates, in hope of transferring his own fiery passion into them. The three mates quail but are not recipient. Some sense of the blasphemy restrains them. Well, if the mates refuse, let the harpooners be exalted, and the mates degraded. The harpooners, savages all, no drop of Christian blood in them, have no hesitation. They are pagan kinsmen and, for the moment, mates of their pagan captain. And now, addressing the reluctant mates, Ahab bids them wait upon their new superiors. "I do appoint ye three cupbearers to my three pagan kinsmen there—yon three most honorable gentlemen and noblemen, my valiant harpooneers." The appointment is declined. "Disdain the task?" continues Ahab. "What, when the great Pope washes the feet of beggars, using his tiara for ewer?" Very well, then; if the mates won't serve, the harpooners will. And they will serve, not in the spirit of obedience, but of their own volition, having been brought under a kind of hypnotic influence. The harpooners represent the emotions and the emotions only; they are therefore easily brought under the sway of a dominant will, as the mates, who have some endowment of rationality, are not. At the very beginning of Ahab's tirade the harpooners responded immediately and enthusiastically, whereas the mates, for a time, hung back. And so Ahab, continuing the spirit of mockery, addresses the harpooners: "Oh, my sweet cardinals! your own condescension, *that* shall bend ye to it. I do not order ye; ye will it. Cut your seizings, and draw the poles, ye harpooneers!"

"Silently obeying the order, the three harpooneers now stood with the detached iron part of their harpoons, some three feet long, held, barbs up, before him." But the irons must be held upside down.

"Cant them; cant them over! know ye not the goblet end? Turn up the socket! So, so; now, ye cup-bearers, advance. The irons! take them; hold them while I fill!" Forthwith, slowly going from one officer to the other, he brimmed the harpoon sockets with the fiery waters from the pewter.

The stage is now set for a "communion with devils," as St. Paul calls it. Ahab is celebrant. "Now, three to three, ye stand. Commend the murderous chalices!

Bestow them, ye who are now made parties to this indissoluble league." At this point Starbuck shows signs of despair or shock. But it's too late now, and Ahab triumphs over the weakling whom he had feared a little while ago. "Ha! Starbuck! but the deed is done! Yon ratifying sun now waits to sit upon it." Then, turning to the harpooners:

"Drink, ye harponeers! drink and swear, ye men that man the deathful whaleboat's bow—Death to Moby Dick! God hunt us all, if we do not hunt Moby Dick to his death!" The long, barbed steel goblets were lifted; and to cries and maledictions against the white whale, the spirits were simultaneously quaffed down with a hiss.

Curses, it will be observed, not prayers. No wonder that Starbuck "paled and turned and shivered." For this is comparable to those "abominations" with which (as Milton says) Baal and other sons of darkness affronted Jehovah's holy rites. "Once more, and finally, the replenished pewter went the rounds among the frantic crew; when, waving his free hand to them, they all dispersed; and Ahab retired within his cabin." Can it be that the waving of the hand is still a mockery, being an imitation of the priest bestowing benediction? In any case, Ahab, in retiring within his cabin, retired from a scene in which he stood as one diabolically possessed, in diabolical possession of his crew.

There is a kind of epilogue to this scene, with the Satanism still more explicit, when, much later, Ahab's own harpoon is forged—forged in hate and tempered in blood. Again the harpooners represent the emotions. In their hot, passionate blood Ahab's purposes are hardened. The blacksmith would temper the harpoon in water, but:

"No, no—no water for that; I want it of the true death-temper. Ahoy, there! Tashtego, Queequeg, Daggoo! What say ye, pagans! Will ye give me as much blood as will cover this barb?" holding it high up. A cluster of dark nods replied, Yes. Three punctures were made in the heathen flesh, and the White Whale's barbs were then tempered.

"Ego non baptizo te in nomine patris, sed in nomine diaboli!" deliriously howled Ahab, as the malignant iron scorchingly devoured the baptismal blood.

To return to the scene of the oath upon the quarter-deck—a promise has been made and solemnized. The mind and will of Ahab have been imposed upon this voyage and have transformed it. It is not an innocent voyage now. The seamen may not know it, but Starbuck does, and he protests. It's a mad project, he insists, mad and blasphemous:

"But what's this long face about, Mr. Starbuck; wilt thou not chase the white whale? art not game for Moby Dick?"

"I am game for his crooked jaw, and for the jaws of Death too, Captain Ahab, if it fairly comes in the way of the business we follow; but I came here to hunt whales, not my commander's vengeance."

Ahab's grandiose and superficial answer does not satisfy. It only provokes another protest:

"Vengeance on a dumb brute!" cried Starbuck, "that simply smote thee from blindest instinct! Madness! To be enraged with a dumb thing, Captain Ahab, seems blasphemous."

Ahab toes the mark. That Starbuck may be satisfied, he will dig a little deeper into his secret motivation. "Hark ye yet again," he cries, "—the little lower layer." This is what the situation now requires; and I shall cut a little wider, if not a little lower, than Ahab does in his argument with Starbuck.

III

Who, it is now pertinent to ask, is this Captain Ahab, the hunter, and what is this Moby Dick, the hunted?

Ahab was born to greatness, even to tragic greatness, and this, the author says, always implies a certain morbidness of character. Symptoms of a tragic destiny appeared in early infancy. Something in his behavior, something not mentioned but easily imagined, revealed to his mother's anxious eye the fatal dower. The man, she foresaw, would be both kingly and blasphemous; he would be an Ahab. And so, to his fatal inheritance she added the fatal increment of a wicked name. The mother's intuition was confirmed by the old squaw Tistig at Gayhead, who said that the name would somehow prove prophetic. So dowered, so named, and subject to such a prophecy, how should he escape the part allotted to him in "the grand programme of Providence that was drawn up a long time ago"?

The mother's intuition was confirmed, again, by Ahab's character and conduct as a whaling captain. The "boiling blood" and the "smoking brow" when a boat was lowered for a whale are not too disquieting; but there was something mysterious and ominous in his temperament, something which Ishmael, lacking the terminology of depth psychology, tries to suggest by the metaphor of deep and dark recesses in the earth. The roots of his nature strike deep down into these lower levels of consciousness. In everything that Ahab does, the unconscious drive is operating upon the conscious purpose; it is this that gives power and plausibility to his character. From this deep source comes his physical and mental energy, both demonic. Little wonder that he perseveres in a course which he knows to be both desperate and mad, that he prefers martyrdom to repentance, that he is proud of the demon that possesses and destroys him.

The fate that the mother dimly apprehended is forecast also in certain outbursts of fury in Ahab's life, prior to this, the final chapter. Elijah, who knows his Ahab, hints darkly at them. Have you not heard, he inquires, "about that thing that happened to him off Cape Horn, long ago, when he lay like dead for three days and nights; nothing about that deadly skrimmage with the Spaniard afore the altar in Santa?—heard nothing about that, eh? Nothing about the silver calabash he spat into?" From these strange fits of passion he recovered, but on the last voyage, in the waters off Japan, he suffered an injury which evoked his fate. A certain white whale, of almost legendary fame for malevolence and ferocity, "dismasted" him:

His three boats stove around him, and oars and men both whirling in the eddies; one captain, seizing the line-knife from his broken prow, had dashed at the whale, as an Arkansas duellist at his foe, blindly seeking with a six inch blade to reach the fathom-deep life of the whale. That captain was Ahab. And then it was, that suddenly sweeping his sickle-shaped lower jaw beneath him, Moby Dick had reaped away Ahab's leg, as a mower a blade of grass in the field.

The dismemberment drove him frantic. For days and weeks and months on the voyage home, "Ahab and anguish lay stretched together in one hammock." Anguish reached such a pitch that Ahab had to be confined in a strait jacket, in which, mad himself, he "swung to the mad rockings of the gales." Finally, the madness subsided into quiet desperation, into a settled, mad resolve to be avenged.

These are the facts. The psychological processes behind them, if discoverable, would make an illuminating page in the book of human nature. Now it so happened that a contemporary of Ahab's, over in Denmark, underwent a variety and extremity of suffering almost, as he thought, unparalleled and then, with an insight almost unparalleled, he analyzed certain problems of suffering, including Ahab's. I refer, of course, to Søren Kierkegaard, some of whose insights I shall make use of.

The problem is despair. The blow falls, in one or another of its countless ways; the suffering seems beyond all measure and desert; the sufferer feels himself singled out—elected, as it were, to be the sport and jest of some malevolent deity. The initial reaction is despair. For a person cut off in this way from the universal pattern and marked out as a sacrifice, there are, says Kierkegaard, two eventualities: he will become demonic or essentially religious.

For a healthy nature there would seem to be release just short of an experience essentially religious. Infinite resignation, as Kierkegaard calls it, even without Christian faith, will bring peace. In the Stoic resignation there was peace, but a hard peace, dictated by pride. There is the example of Diogenes, of whom Epictetus says: "Hadst thou seized upon his possessions, he would rather have let them go than have followed thee for them—aye, had it been even a limb." But Ahab was too passionate and self-willed to make the gesture of infinite resignation. From a child he had been rebellious. The Stoic could submit himself to Providence. He could knit his mutilated spirit into the spirit of the universe. But not Ahab. "Who's over me?" he demands of Starbuck, in response to an expostulation. Stubb, who knew him well, reports that he never saw him kneel.

There remains the Christian way of resignation, the only way, according to Kierkegaard, whereby a morbid nature, passionate and self-willed, can encounter despair and conquer it. If the sufferer can say: "Before thee, O God, I am nothing, do with me as thou wilt," he will be able to bear the burden. He can lose the self, and then, by the well-known Christian paradox, regain it. But of Christian feeling there is no trace in Ahab. All the ways of resignation are therefore closed.

The alternative, in Kierkegaard's analysis, is defiance. Since the sufferer cannot lose himself, his one recourse is to affirm himself. The despair is not thereby cured. There is despair in the very effort to combat despair. As the consciousness of self increases, the despair increases, while the increasing despair increases the consciousness of self. The cycle thus set in motion has an inevitable outcome: the sufferer becomes demonic.

An important stage in Ahab's progress from the blind rage of complete despair to a rage partially subdued and organized under mad direction is reached in an incident which occurred before the "Pequod" sailed, although it is not described until long afterward. It is postponed, I suppose, in order that the element of allegory might readily be perceived. Ahab had returned home, the "Pequod" was getting ready, when one night he fell and was discovered lying upon the ground, helpless and insensible. "His ivory limb [had] been so violently displaced, that it had stake-wise smitten, and all but pierced his groin; nor was it without extreme difficulty that the agonizing wound was entirely cured." In this incident we find that Moby Dick—present in the ivory stake—had bitten into the very center of his being, leaving a wound that was to prove incurable. But Kierkegaard would see something more—a push toward the demonic. The incident included a twofold psychic trauma—the initial humiliation in his own eyes and the subsequent humiliation arising from compassion on the part of others. To be lifted out of the universal pattern, to be an object of humiliation to one's self and an object of compassion to others—this torture, more than any other, says Kierkegaard, tempts man to rebel against God. It can be borne only by resignation. But if it is combined with a passionate self-will, "then it will end with the sufferer losing his reason." As an instance of self-will turning the sufferer demonic, Kierkegaard cites Richard III. Of despair referred to God and turning into triumph, he is his own example. In the case of Ahab, it was this fall, hushed up by the few friends who knew about it, that sent him into a lama-like seclusion in his cabin—a seclusion from which he did not emerge until, turned demonic, he took his place upon the quarter-deck, prepared and determined to league his crew into a solemn oath to seek revenge upon Moby Dick.

And now, what of Moby Dick, the hunted?

He is a more mysterious being than Ahab, the hunter.

On the level of plain fact he is simply a legendary white whale, the object of an exciting chase. On the level of allegory he is the presence of evil in the world, and his whiteness is both essential and mysterious. It was on the voyage home that Moby Dick was transformed from the particular to the universal, from fact to symbol:

> All that most maddens and torments; all that stirs up the lees of things; all truth with malice in it; all that cracks the sinews and cakes the brain; all the subtle demonisms of life and thought; all evil, to crazy Ahab, were visibly personified, and made practically assailable in Moby Dick. He piled upon the whale's white hump the sum of all the general rage and hate felt by his whole race from Adam down; and then, as if his chest had been a mortar, he burst his hot heart's shell upon it.

It is as if, in the turmoil of Ahab's mind, an ancient superstition had risen into consciousness—the superstition of the scapegoat. Upon the head of an innocent animal were placed symbolically the sins of the whole community, and the animal was then sanctified and slain. But the object of Ahab's pursuit is the whole world's scapegoat, laden in his imagination with the whole world's evil. There is a difference, however, between the primitive scapegoat and Moby Dick. For Moby Dick is not an innocent animal bearing the world's evil; he is, in Ahab's sight, the evil without the innocence, and without the sanctification. The slaying of him, therefore, cannot be redemptive. This Ahab does not clearly see. He believes, or half-believes, that vengeance may have a redemptive quality. Mistaken as he is, however, Moby Dick has been transformed, in his imagination, from fact to symbol, though without losing, for the crew, his identity as a fact. The story moves on both levels to the end. The "unearthly conceit that Moby Dick was ubiquitous; that he had actually been encountered in opposite latitudes at one and the same instant of time," suggests the ubiquity of evil; but, at the same time, there is an effort, surely strained, to make the conceit plausible in fact. The reports of some whalers that Moby Dick was not only ubiquitous but immortal, that, "though groves of spears should be planted in his flanks, he would still swim away unharmed"—this report, on the allegorical level, is too obvious to state. More subtle is the report that Moby Dick's ferocity often seems deliberate, conscious, and intelligent. (How often we feel like saying that when the blow falls!) The terror he inspires is such that some think him supernatural or nearly so, and the terror seems to lie mainly in his color. His wrinkled brow is snow-white, and he carries a vast white hump. This "grand hooded phantom, like a snow hill in the air," is the mysterious monster that Ishmael went to sea to behold and ponder over. This is the devil incarnate that Ahab has willed to wrestle with and slay.

The supreme element in the terror Moby Dick inspires—his dazzling whiteness—is a mystery so baffling that Ishmael, who discourses on it, takes up the theme with a sense of inevitable failure. He says:

Aside from those more obvious considerations touching Moby Dick, which could not but occasionally awaken in any man's soul some alarm, there was another thought, or rather vague, nameless horror concerning him, which at times by its intensity completely overpowered all the rest; and yet so mystical and well nigh ineffable was it, that I almost despair of putting it in a comprehensible form.

It was the whiteness of the whale that above all things appalled me. But how can I hope to explain myself here; and yet, in some dim, random way, explain myself I must, else all these chapters might be naught.

I, too, must take up this burden, for we have Ishmael's plain word for it that the central meaning of the book lies in this chapter.

The core of the chapter is simply this: that white is capable of two contrary effects. On the one hand, it is the emblem of innocence, honor, and purity; of the mystery of justice and the beauty of holiness; of whatever, in short, is sweet and honorable and sublime. On the other hand, it expresses the deepest terror that man knows; it is a bleak and desolate color; it is instinctively associated with the world's malevolence. There is a gigantic ghastliness in the wind-blown snows of the prairies, in the white scenery of the Antarctic, in the snow-capped mountains. It is a strange paradox that the same color should be "at once the most meaning symbol of spiritual things, nay, the very veil of the Christian's Deity; and yet should be as it is, the intensifying agent in things the most appalling to mankind." Divested of its investiture in white, it is the paradox of good and evil being ultimately one.

But, when the white inheres in the white whale, and particularly in its white hump, rising up like a snow hill in the air, the color and its paradox become alive, with a life keyed into the mystery and majesty of the great Leviathan. Here now, in a superlative degree, is an image of the kind beloved by contemporary poets, one expressing a whole complex of thought and emotion and fusing, in this instance, a variety of opposites, such as beauty and desolation, holiness and demonism, what is of good report and what of bad—more simply, good and evil. For some readers the symbol would carry a still deeper significance. For them the mysterious fusion of those contraries in Moby Dick would be but a reflection, in the somewhat deceptive world of sense, of the union of moral contraries, and, indeed, of all contraries, in the world of ultimate reality. The Hindus, for example, believe that the contraries are united in Brahma and in Krishna, his avatar. The following lines refer to Krishna:

> I heard the passion breathed amid the honeysuckle
>   scented glade,
> And saw the King pass lightly from the beauty that
>   he had betrayed.
> I saw him pass from love to love; and yet the pure
>   allowed his claim
> To be the purest of the pure, thrice holy, stainless,
>   without blame.

That, as the reader has probably recognized, is "A. E.," and here he is in prose:

The sphere of the argumentative intellect is the world where all things exist by way of balance of opposites, where for every black there is a white, and for every *pro* a *con;* and, if we lived only by the intellect, there could be no progress, for argument could be met by equal argument. "An eye for an eye, and a tooth for a tooth" is the justice of the intellect, and that warfare may go on for ever. We can only escape from an eternity of opposites by rising above them like that spirit which fixed the balance in the heavens and made equal centrifugal and centripetal. It was that spirit which would fain have admitted man to its own sphere, showing how to escape from the dominion of the opposites by rising above them. It counselled forgiveness until seventy times seven—a hard saying, no doubt, to those who have just cause for offence. But it is the only way by which we can be melted and made one in the higher spheres....

Similarly, Blake asked, in a famous poem, whether it was possible to believe that he who made the lamb also made the tiger. Not only possible but necessary. And the first article of Blake's message to the world is this: Inquire not into the mystery of good and evil. To separate them apart and brood over them—to bring them under the scrutiny of a doubting head and a selfish heart is to open the gates of hell. By this action Adam fell; by this action the children of Adam have been falling to this day.

Since "A. E." and Blake are commonly called "mystics," I must disavow any intention of implying that Ahab and Ishmael were such. Yet it may be said that the turmoil in Ahab's mind on the voyage home opened up a very deep rift of consciousness through which he saw an age-old symbol, one akin to those which Jung calls "archetypal," and one of whose subtlety he was but partially aware. And it may be also that Ishmael, in his effort to fathom what was going on in Ahab's mind, reached far beyond his usual grasp. Ordinarily, the truth for Ishmael is the truth of Solomon and Ecclesiastes; yet he can pass into cosmic consciousness, though he distrusts the experience. I do not know how much it means, but it is pertinent to recall the fact that when Ishmael first catches sight of the wondrous white whale, which he had thought of as "the gliding great demon of the seas of life" and as "that demon phantom that, some time or other, swims before all human hearts," the story of "the white bull Jupiter swimming away with ravished Europa clinging to his graceful horns" comes to his mind, bringing to the demon a touch of divinity. Had Ishmael, in his reflections upon Ahab's quest, not descried a truth far beyond his usual horizon, why did he fumble and stumble in his effort to report it and feel so keenly the inadequacy of his report?

However, Ishmael's somewhat mysterious speculations upon the mystery of good and evil do not have to be understood as a mystic would understand them. If it be admitted that the duality of good and evil is veiled in the unity of white, so that one cannot be sure of their separate identity, it is enough. "It was from out the rind of one apple tasted," wrote Milton in the *Areopagitica*, "that the knowledge of good and evil as two twins cleaving together, leaped forth into the world. And perhaps this is the doom which Adam fell into of knowing good and evil, that is to say, of knowing good by evil." The children of Adam are doomed to see these twins in separation. The danger is that separation should fall into hostility, the one twin being seen as a child of light, the other as a child of darkness. Prevention, in so far as this can be prevented, lies in the recognition that the moral struggle is not altogether in our hands, that good is somehow more real than evil, that no person, cause, or institution is wholly guiltless, and that the final mystery of evil is beyond human comprehension. To lose this minimum of faith is to be in danger of going Ahab's way.

Not to see the problem at all is Starbuck's way—at least, not to see it clearly enough to understand Ahab. To see the problem eye to eye with Ahab, and yet withhold a vengeful hand, is Ishmael's way. Ishmael, who is both troubled and comforted by the paradox of white, is a man of only a minimum of faith; but this minimum, together with a great deal of common sense, is sufficient to tell him that Ahab is mad. Yet he understands Ahab's madness perfectly, and easily thinks Ahab's thoughts. As his meditations upon white draw to an end, they drift, unconsciously, it would seem, to Ahab's point of view. Reflecting upon the fact that white is the sum of all the colors and, at the same time, a kind of "visible absence of color," Ishmael toys with the morbid fancy that the gay and lovely hues with which so many objects are invested are but subtle deceits and that, if we could lift the painted veil, the palsied universe would lie before us with the whiteness of a leper. This, indeed, is how it does look to the eye of "the wretched infidel." To his gaze the world seems wrapped in a "monumental white shroud." But the "wretched infidel" of this passage is Ahab, not Ishmael. The faith of Ishmael is small, no greater than a mustard seed, but it is enough to stay his hand and to save him, in the end, sole and single among a crew that had even less faith than he.

Of all the children of Adam who have set the twins of good and evil in violent opposition, none have surpassed the Parsees, that is to say, the Persians. First, there were the disciples of Zoroaster. For them the world was a stage for the warfare of good and evil, the principle of good (and light) being personified in Ahura-Mazda, the principle of evil (and darkness) in Ahriman. For some thousands of years, it was believed, the warfare would continue, now with one side winning, now the other; but in the end good and light would triumph. Meanwhile, the summons to all men was to a life militant in the service of Ahura-Mazda. Still, every man was free to choose. Among those who chose the good, the supreme object of worship was fire. The sacred flame, elaborately protected from contamination, burned in every temple. Of this religion there are few adherents now, these being mainly the Parsees of Bombay, in whose temples the sacred flame still burns. But Parsism entered a second and final phase in Manichaeism. Originating in Persia, in the third century of the Christian Era, it traveled far to the west (as well as to the east), winning countless adherents; for its picture of a self-divided world made sense to a world that had fallen into inner self-division. A modern scholar, observing that the Greek epoch of spiritual habitation had passed, by St. Augustine's time, into an epoch of spiritual homelessness, asserts that Augustine asked in a new way the old question, "What is man, that Thou art mindful of him?" He continues:

The solitude out of which he asked the question can only be understood when one realizes that that round and unified world of Aristotle had long since collapsed. It collapsed because the soul of man, divided against itself, could no longer grasp as truth anything but a world which was divided against itself. In place of the sphere which had collapsed there now arose two autonomous and mutually hostile kingdoms, the kingdom of light and the kingdom of darkness. We meet them again in almost every system of that widespread and manifold spiritual movement of gnosis, which at that time seized the embarrassed heirs of the great oriental and antique cultures, split the godhead and emptied value from creation; and in the most consistent of these systems, in Manichaeism, there is even, consistently, a double earth.

Such was the Parsee mind and the Parsee world. But wiser minds have striven for integration, inward and outward. Therefore, a sounder instinct was at work in Jacob Boehme, who recognized the warring opposites but brought them into unity, at least in theory, by thinking of them as the two parts of a flame. There is the dark base of fire—the wrath—God the Father; and there is the tip of light—the forgiveness—Christ the Son. As the light tip is generated out of the dark base, as the darkness is the necessary food or fuel of the light, so Christ the Son is perpetually generated out of God the Father. The two are organic parts of one. I mention this theory of Boehme's because the imagery of fire and light, as well as of light and darkness, has so often occurred to the mind of man pondering over the problem of good and evil; and because in this very book the symbolism of white, as a mysterious emblem of this duality, often yields to the symbolism of light and darkness and of light and fire.

Ishmael, on one occasion, very nearly lost his ship by contemplating its activities under the light of fire. It was night, and he was standing at the helm, fascinated by the scene below, where the try-works smoked and blazed with the blubber of a luckless whale tossed into them by a savage, hilarious crew:

As they narrated to each other their unholy adventures, their tales of terror told in words of mirth; as their uncivilized laughter forked upwards out of them, like the flames from the furnace; as to and fro, in their front, the harpooneers wildly gesticulated with their huge pronged forks and dippers; as the wind howled on, and the sea leaped, and the ship groaned and dived, and yet steadfastly shot her red hell further and further into the blackness of the sea and the night, and scornfully champed the white bone in her mouth, and viciously spat round her on all sides; then the rushing Pequod, freighted with savages, and laden with fire, and burning a corpse, and plunging into that blackness of darkness, seemed the material counterpart of her monomaniac commander's soul.

As Ishmael gazed at this grim scene and meditated upon its moral counterpart, he passed into a state of semiconsciousness and forgot his compass. Recovering just in time to avert disaster, he found that he had turned himself about and was facing backward. He found, also, that his own action had a moral counterpart:

Look not too long in the face of the fire, O man! Never dream with thy hand on the helm! Turn not thy back to the compass; accept the first hint of the hitching tiller; believe not the artificial fire, when its redness makes all things look ghastly. Tomorrow, in the natural sun, the skies will be bright; those who glared like devils in the forking flames, the morn will show in far other, at least gentler, relief; the glorious, golden, glad sun, the only true lamp— all others but liars!

The light in Ahab's soul regressed to fire on the voyage home. The moral world, under his fiery apprehension of it, split asunder—into a principle of light and a principle of darkness, a principle of light and a principle of fire. At the same time, the fire in his own heart burned for vengeance upon the fiery torment of the world:

The White Whale swam before him as the monomaniac incarnation of all those malicious agencies which some deep men feel eating in them, till they are left living on with half a heart and half a lung. That intangible malignity which has been from the beginning; to whose dominion even the modern Christians ascribe one-half of the worlds; which the ancient Ophites of the east reverenced in their statue devil;—Ahab did not fall down and worship it like them; but deliriously transferring its idea to the abhorred white whale, he pitted himself, all mutilated, against it.

Captain Ahab has done something very like what King Ahab did before him. He has permitted a false god to enter his domain of consciousness, a Parsee Ahriman to challenge a Parsee Mazda. And he has taken up the challenge, not in the spirit of an enlightened Parsee, but with a fiery passion that in the course of time will make the hellish scene just described seem like an external counterpart of the hell within.

IV

I return, after this long digression, to the "Pequod" and the scene of that diabolical communion upon the quarter-deck. That the whole crew should be persuaded to take the oath, all of them becoming Ahabs, as their commander said, was a thing incredible to expect and triumphant to accomplish. But Ahab found, reviewing it, that " 'Twas not so hard a task. I thought to find one stubborn, at the least"; but that one—Starbuck— had weakly given in. It must therefore be with mingled feelings—disdain as well as triumph—that Ahab exclaims: "Ha! Starbuck! but the deed is done! Yon ratifying sun now waits to sit upon it." Oh, the measureless irony in that word "ratifying"! It is not the sun, seeming to pause upon the horizon, but the oncoming night, that ratifies the deed. The doer and the deed have both been registered, one might say, in the kingdom of darkness, where inexorable consequences have already been set in motion.

This Ahab knows full well, and he goes down to his cabin to accept, with mingled defiance and despair, the price of his recent triumph. A bit of exultation still remains. "My soul mounts up!" he declares defiantly—mounts up in contrast with the sun, "slow dived from noon." But exultation gives way immediately to exhaustion, and defiance to despair: "She wearies with the endless hill." This is the hill that he has been climbing against the voice of conscience ever since the "Pequod" sailed—a hill that will continue to mount as he mounts, creating defiance and despair alternately.

In this scene despair, on the whole, comes first. A mortal man against the gods—could even iron sinews endure that struggle? "Is, then, the crown too heavy that I wear? this Iron Crown of Lombardy?" A saying of Captain Peleg's comes to mind. "*He's Ahab*, boy; and Ahab of old, thou knowest, was a crowned king!" Our Ahab also has assumed a crown. If the analogy had occurred to Ahab at this moment, it would have induced somber thoughts. But it is safe to say that the recollection of other kings occupied his mind—those sovereigns who had assumed the jeweled crown of Lombardy, among whom were Napoleon and Charlemagne. And then, borne in on a tide of anguish, the recollection of another king—the king of the Jews, who died upon the cross. For Ahab, knowing of the crown of Lombardy, knew that the narrow iron band inside it was supposed to have been made from a nail used at the Crucifixion. This granted, it hardly seems farfetched to discern the crown of thorns pressing for recognition. His crown hurts, and hurts in a special way. " 'Tis iron—that I know—not gold. 'Tis split, too

—that I feel; the jagged edge galls me so, my brain seems to beat against the solid metal." At the image of the Crucifixion, Ahab would not have flinched. The mind that conceived and carried through the scene upon the quarter-deck could take the consequences. Besides, did he not know that the red-hot iron crown had been a martyr's crown, and was he not ready to die, if need be, for the cause? Pride, defiance, despair—but who could disentangle and define the whole complex of emotion at this great moment when he deliberately assumed the crown of responsibility? If the crown is heavy, "yet is it bright with many a gem; I, the wearer, see not its far flashings; but darkly feel that I wear that, that dazzlingly confounds." But the end of it all is defiance and despair. Something tells him that the quality of his martyrdom is not pure; it is adulterated with selfishness, it is nothing less than mad. Another saying of Captain Peleg's comes to mind: "No, no, my lad; stricken, blasted, if he be, Ahab has his humanities!" They are burning low now, like the waning light outside, but they are not extinguished; they still provide sufficient light to illuminate the darkness of Ahab's soul. They move him, however, only to grief, not to repentance, repentance being blocked by a sense of the tragic grandeur in his course. The grief is the loss of his enjoying power. The light of sunset no longer soothes him:

This lovely light, it lights not me; all loveliness is anguish to me, since I can ne'er enjoy. Gifted with the high perception, I lack the low, enjoying power; damned, most subtly and most malignantly! damned in the midst of Paradise!

To that darkening paradise he waves his hand and says good-night. In that word, spoken in full understanding of the issue and acceptance of the outcome—in that word and the gesture which accompanies it—a whole tragedy is distilled.

The anguish that Ahab felt as he gazed upon the no longer ratifying sun, and contrasted the life within with the life without, had been felt by Coleridge:

> All this long eve, so balmy and serene,
> Have I been gazing on the western sky,
>   And its peculiar tint of yellow green;
> And still I gaze—and with how blank an eye! . . .
>
> O Lady! we receive but what we give,
> And in our life alone does Nature live.

The reason in each case could be stated in St. Paul's words, a little altered: The eyes of the heart were darkened. Why this darkening? Ahab understood his own case, as he thought, and the reasons, as far as they go, are right: Gifted with the high perception, lacking the low, enjoying power. This, less acutely, is also Ivan's situation in *The Brothers Karamazov*. He, too, has taken the intellectual approach and becomes rebellious. Finding the earth soaked from crust to center with the tears of humanity, he finds the scheme of things intolerable and is preparing to give his ticket back. But he is not rebellious, as Ahab is, to the point of complete incommunication; he can therefore listen to Alyosha's counsel, which is to love everything in the world:

"Love life more than the meaning of it?"

"Certainly, love it, regardless of logic as you say, it must be regardless of logic, and it's only then one will understand the meaning of it."

In spite of his rebelliousness, Ivan still loves "the sticky little leaves as they open in spring." But Alyosha is fearful lest he lose all:

"But the little sticky leaves, and the precious tombs, and the blue sky, and the woman you love! How will you live, how will you love them?" Alyosha cried sorrowfully. "With such a hell in your heart and your head, how can you?"

This is Ahab's case precisely. Not gifted with the low perception, he has never started with the neighbor, with little children, with the lowly and the immediate. With such a beginning, no limit is set upon the embrace of love. It does not begin with the high perception, or, if it does, it is likely to be sterile. All this Ahab doubtless knew. He had read it in the Gospels, certainly, but with as blank an eye as that which scanned the sunset.

The sense of being damned, subtly and malignantly— this is despair; but it gives way immediately to renewed defiance: "What I've dared, I've willed; and what I've willed, I'll do!" But the surviving humanities, sitting in judgment upon their master, tell him pitilessly that what he has willed to do is mad. "They think me mad— Starbuck does; but I'm demoniac, I am madness maddened! That wild madness that's only calm to comprehend itself!" And then he proves the soundness of his diagnosis in a burst of wild and whirling words in which his soul mounts up in a self-affirmation which is but the compensation of a corresponding self-despair:

I laugh and hoot at ye, [ye gods], ye cricket-players, ye pugilists, ye deaf Burkes and blinded Bendigoes! I will not say as schoolboys do to bullies,—Take some one of your own size; don't pommel *me!* No, ye've knocked me down, and I am up again; but *ye* have run and hidden. Come forth from behind your cotton bags! I have no long gun to reach ye. Come, Ahab's compliments to ye; come and see if ye can swerve me.

They cannot swerve him because they are subject to necessity as well as he. And his necessity is to push on like a locomotive, which, a hundred years ago, was the ultimate in determination:

Swerve me? ye cannot swerve me, else ye swerve yourselves! man has ye there. Swerve me? The path to my fixed purpose is laid with iron rails, whereon my soul is grooved to run. Over unsounded gorges, through the rifled hearts of mountains, under torrents' beds, unerringly I rush! Naught's an obstacle, naught's an angle to the iron way!

That is demonic. It is a quality of mind and will explained by Kierkegaard as arising from the presense in despair and defiance of the element of the eternal. The presence of the eternal in Ahab (or of the same thing by another name, if the reader wishes) is insistent. Ishmael recognized it: "Oh, Ahab! what shall be grand in thee, it must needs be plucked at from the skies, and dived for in the deep, and featured in the unbodied air!" It is this quality that, in Ahab's words, maddens madness. Kierkegaard's description of the sufferer and the suffering is so penetrating that it points straight at Ahab:

But the more consciousness [of the eternal] there is in such a sufferer who in despair is determined to be himself, all the more does despair too potentiate itself and become demoniac. The genesis of this is commonly as follows. A self which in despair is determined to be itself winces at one pain or another which simply cannot be taken away or separated from its concrete self. Precisely upon this torment the man directs his whole passion, which at last becomes a demoniac rage. Even if at this point God in heaven and all his angels were to offer to help him out of it—no, now he doesn't want it, now it is too late, he once would have given everything to be rid of this torment but was made to wait, now that's all past, now he would rather rage against everything, he, the one man in the whole of existence who is the most unjustly treated, to whom it is especially important to have his torment at hand, important that no one should take it from him—for thus he can convince himself that he is in the right. . . . Revolting against the whole of existence, [the sufferer] thinks [he] has hold of a proof against it, against its goodness. This proof the despairer thinks he himself is, and that is what he wills to be, therefore he wills to be himself, himself with his torment, in order with this torment to protest against the whole of existence.

This passage might be illustrated in detail from Ahab's history. The element of the eternal is felt in every word and at every step. It has appeared already in the crucifixion in Ahab's face when first he took his stand upon the quarter-deck, in the superhuman power of will which imposed the oath, in the blasphemy of the diabolical communion, in the desperation of the ensuing despair, in the assumption of the iron crown. It has appeared also in the demonic will power which Ahab imposed upon the initial hysteria, subduing those turbulent emotions and organizing them under mad direction. Ishmael's account of what happened at that juncture is in harmony with Kierkegaard:

Human madness is oftentimes a cunning and most feline thing. When you think it fled, it may have but become transfigured into some still subtler form. Ahab's full lunacy subsided not, but deepeningly contracted; like the unabated Hudson, when that noble Northman flows narrowly, but unfathomably through the Highland gorge.

But, as in his narrow-flowing monomania, not one jot of Ahab's broad madness had been left behind; so in that broad madness, not one jot of his great natural intellect had perished. That before living agent, now became the living instrument. If such a furious trope may stand, his special lunacy stormed his general sanity, and carried it, and turned all its concentred cannon upon its own mad mark; so that far from having lost his strength, Ahab, to that one end, did now posses a thousand fold more potency than ever he had sanely brought to bear upon any one reasonable object.

But this strength is countered by another strength, less strong than the maddened one, yet strong enough to constitute rebellion. Ahab could say, as Faust does, "Two souls, alas, dwell in my breast apart." A psychiatrist would say that he had suffered a neurosis. The conflict is indicated by the alternating or simultaneously contending moods of defiance and despair; but these are symptoms rather than causes. Nearer to causes would be an understanding of the conflict suggested by Captain Peleg's statement that Ahab, "blasted, if he be . . . has his humanities." The struggle would then be one between humanities and inhumanities.

For the inhumanities a single sentence will suffice: "He was intent on an audacious, immitigable and supernatural revenge." The humanities, however, have to be sought out. Moreover, the case for them at this early stage of Ahab's progress can be but partial. Nevertheless, the conditions of the neurosis can be suggested.

The humanities must at all times be apprehended mainly by a sense of presence, not palpably. They are the disturbing factor which keeps the neurosis going. It is they that give Ahab the full consciousness from first to last that he is mad. They are the voice of conscience, impotent except as torment, before his sense of fate. They extort an occasional confession:—Why bother about the leaking casks? "I'm all aleak myself." They are an element in the fiery visions which drive him screaming from his bed. They are the source of the crucifixion in his face when first he takes command, and of the crucifixion in his heart when he assumes the iron crown. They are the agents of his despair. Without his humanities, Ahab would be a god or a beast; yet he is neither. He is what Captain Peleg says he is, "a grand, ungodly, god-like man."

But the humanities have also a definite and beneficent influence. They mitigate, to some extent, that implacable revenge, by giving it an intellectual, even a metaphysical, quality. What is this thing, asks Ahab, on which I have to avenge myself? Is evil in the appearance, the painted veil, the pasteboard masks, or is it some intangible thing behind appearances?

But in each event—in the living act, the undoubted deed—there, some unknown but still reasoning thing puts forth the mouldings of its features from behind the unreasoning mask. If man will strike, strike through the mask! How can the prisoner reach outside except by thrusting through the wall? To me, the white whale is that wall, shoved near to me.

But there are times when it would seem that appearances are all. "Sometimes I think there's naught beyond." However that may be, the image of the whale possesses his imagination:

He tasks me; he heaps me; I see in him outrageous strength, with an inscrutable malice sinewing it. That inscrutable thing is chiefly what I hate; and be the white whale agent, or be the white whale principal, I will wreak that hate upon him.

If Starbuck thinks this blasphemy, let him think so. "Talk not to me of blasphemy, man; I'd strike the sun if it insulted me."

It is a miracle that this story of implacable revenge should take on a philosophic coloring; that this simple Nantucket sailor, whose intellectual prowess is nevertheless often insisted on, should actually seem to be engaged, to some extent, upon a philosophic quest. The degree of modification is something that each reader must decide for himself, but he can hardly deny that it is there. Ahab's distraught but still reflective mind breaks forth in soliloquy and ejaculation, in defiance and despair, in response, as time increases tension, to the slightest provocation. His intellectual stature grows with the story's growth; it cannot be adequately measured now.

The revenge motive is modified in still another way. Ishmael tells us that Ahab identified the whale not only with his bodily woes but with his intellectual and spiritual exasperations, and to his own he added the exasperations of all mankind. In avenging himself, he is, in a way, avenging the whole world. Thus he acquires a sense of martyrdom. His crown, in part at least a martyr's crown, is bright with many a gem, it flashes far, it dazzlingly confounds. The assumption of a crown of hate is a perversion of true devotion to mankind. Ahab does not bring to his defiance Prometheus' purity of mind or Job's purity of heart; but his sense of devotion to a cause, partial and perverted as it is, lifts his vengeance above the petty and the personal and gives it a tragic dignity.

V

The first stage of the neurosis was the hysteria consequent upon dismemberment. Then came control; first outward—a strait jacket; then inward—a plan. The plan was not a cure for the hysteria, it only checked and channeled it and offered a prospect of eventual release. In its cunning and its daring it preserved the original neurosis, since it was nothing less than for Ahab to gain control, by subversive means, of a whaling ship and turn it into his private battle cruiser for the pursuit of Moby Dick.

As the plan enters Ahab's mind, there enters also the agent of the plan, the Parsee. Not yet outward and visible, he will be a sinister figure when he does appear, a Mephistopheles returned to seduce another Faust. But the Parsee is not really an external agent, sent to tempt a certain victim by arrangement with the Lord; he is the creation of Ahab's own self-seducing mind. This means a doubting mind, a doubting Puritan or Parsee mind, and such a mind wilfully and passionately concerned with the moral problems of a dual world.

By a "Puritan or Parsee mind" I mean one which draws sharp lines of moral separation. The Parsees drew such a line between good and evil. The Puritans drew many such lines, their minds being characterized, as Ralph Barton Perry has remarked, by "an irreconcilable yes or no." From these divisions sprang the Puritans' moral zeal and the dangerous assumption that God was on their side of the line, Satan on the other. This is the kind of world recalled by Henry Adams:

Resistance to something was the law of New England nature; the boy looked out on the world with the instinct of resistance; for numberless generations his predecessors had viewed the world chiefly as a thing to be reformed, filled with evil forces to be abolished, and they saw no reason to suppose that they had wholly succeeded in the abolition; the duty was unchanged. That duty implied not only resistance to evil, but hatred of it. Boys naturally look on all force as an enemy, and generally find it so, but the New Englander, whether boy or man, in his long struggle with a stingy or hostile universe, had learned also to love the pleasure of hating; his joys were few.

Such was the normal Puritan outlook. It had been Ahab's outlook for forty years. A world definitely divided into good and evil; a life definitely on the side of good; a joyless life except for the pleasure of hating the precious whale; a life of honorable trade, construed, as the Puritans did construe it, as having a religious quality. In reviewing that long period, Ahab speaks of it both as Parsee and as Puritan. "Oh! thou clear spirit of clear fire, whom on these seas I as Persian once did worship, till in the sacramental act so burned by thee, that to this hour I bear the scar. . . ." There speak both righteousness and self-righteousness. A perfect and upright man in his own eyes, he is made to Satan's hand, could Satan but get permission to try Ahab as he tried Job. We can imagine Satan, having chosen his victim more shrewdly this time, saying to the Lord: "Put forth thy hand now and touch his bone and flesh, and he will renounce thee to thy face." Bone and flesh were touched; Satan's (imaginary) prediction was fulfilled.

Job was saved by humility and faith. Humility need not be mentioned relative to Ahab. On the contrary, there was a sleeping demon in him which had been roused to fury more than once. There were pride and passion related to that demon and related also to the daring and dangers of his trade. Self-righteousness was basic. As for his faith, it reeled under the physical penalty. The game of life as he understood it had been broken into and broken up. He had thought of himself as a good soldier in the secular service of the Lord, and the Lord he had conceived of as a stern commander, like himself, but one from whom fair play could be expected. "I'd strike the sun it if insulted me. For could the sun do that, then could I do the other; since there is ever a sort of fair play herein, jealousy presiding over all creations." Well, fair play is over now. The penalty of a leg was foul play, not fair; the game of life has reverted to the primitive blood feud—an eye for an eye, a tooth for a tooth.

Yet not without opposition from Ahab's humanities. Revenge planned as Ahab planned it passed all rational, moral, and religious bounds. A portion of Ahab's mind therefore rose in opposition, thus forming a cleavage and laying the foundation of a neurosis. At least three voices spoke in protest. Reason: the plan is madness. Conscience: the plan is blasphemous. Fear: the plan is impossible. Did love and forgiveness ever speak? It will appear in due course that they did, finding a voice in Pip. Until then the humanities were unorganized and hence unable to summon Ahab to a solemn and decisive judgment. They could only create a continual disturbance.

The subtly maddened half of Ahab's mind is represented by the Parsee. Initially, this mind is doubt, a mind which sees the world as a theater of war between good and evil but has lost faith in the outcome, and even in the high command. But doubt, which is one form of selfhood, striking into wilful emotions, which are another form, is only the first step in a fatal progress. Kierkegaard understood that progress, and so did Blake. It is not surprising, therefore, that the Parsee should call to mind certain figures of Blake's myth, especially Urizen and the Spectre. These figures represent the reasoning power divorced from faith and consequently from all the virtues of the life of imagination. They draw their victim first into doubt, then into selfhood and despair. Selfhood, struggling with despair, engenders Satanic pride. Release can only come by annihilation of the selfhood and a return, through faith, to the life of imagination.

That doubt had entered Ahab's wilful mind would be a safe deduction from many circumstances, but there is also a positive statement. It is definitely said of the Parsee not only that he is one of those mysterious orientals whom the inhabitants of the temperate zones see only in their dreams but that he preserved, even in these modern days, the consciousness of earth's primal generations—the generations when men first were asking the primal questions of whence and why and whither. Ahab preserves the racial consciousness in various ways, and among them in this: that he too was asking these primal questions, not only with the curious mind, but with the passionate blood, and setting the particular question of good and evil and the dangerous Parsee relationship of independent and sovereign powers.

But the Parsee also recalls Mephistopheles. His dress is as picturesque as the dress of Mephistopheles, and certain inner qualities—the self-assurance, the deceit, and trickery—are identical. These inner qualities, whose potentialities Ahab does not fully comprehend, are really traits of the type of mind that now possesses him; but their projection into a concrete living character makes them vivid and dramatic. To Stubb, the protruding tooth suggests a snake's head; one thing and another suggest a tail; he's no mortal, certainly—he's ageless; he's up to some trick or other, signed a bond with Ahab, maybe, to kidnap him or get his soul. In these fancies the devil and Mephistopheles come together; but the Parsee, in so far as he is Mephistopheles, is an oriental one, silent, passionless, fatalistic.

The Parsee is accompanied by four shadowy figures, who are nameless and comparatively unimportant. The five of them go aboard the "Pequod," as nearly as possible with Ahab and unseen of all but Ishmael, among the crew. On the sailing day we are told that "the captain came aboard last night." But when dawn broke gray and misty, Ishmael thought he discerned some shadowy figures running toward the boat, and his suspicion was confirmed by Elijah, who appears a second time to utter a second warning. "Did ye see anything looking like men going towards that ship a while ago?" And then he adds, significantly, "See if you can find 'em now, will ye?" Days pass before they are found, and they are heard before they are seen. Mysterious sounds issue from the hold—now something like a cough, now something like sleepers turning over. Later on we learn that Ahab made many a visit down below. "Aye," says Stubb, "and that's what he went into the after hold for, so often, as Dough-Boy long suspected.

They were hidden down there. The White Whale's at the bottom of it." Stubb—simple, jolly Stubb—frequently has gleams of insight. Yes, the white whale was at the bottom of it, and these nocturnal sessions were between Ahab and his Spectre, between that part of Ahab's mind which still was troubled by the protests of his "humanities" and that part—personified in the Parsee—which rationalized his projected vengeance. Whenever the mind contemplates an evil course, there must be a period of doubt and hesitation, unless all conscience has been lost. But the reasoning mind, if not regulated by benevolent emotions, is a great deceiver. This thing you call vengeance, it will say, is really justice, you can do it safely, you will never be found out, you will have settled your score, and you will find peace at last. In such wise, we may suppose, did the Parsee argue with what was left of Ahab's Puritan morality. When, at last, doubt and hesitation were subdued and Ahab, on deck, imposed the oath of vengeance upon his crew, there came "the low laugh from the hold," a mocking, malevolent, Mephistophelean laugh—the signal of the Parsee's triumph. When a protest came from Starbuck, "the subterranean laugh died away," but the protest was short-lived, and Ahab embraced his fate.

Thus triumphant, the Parsee can appear on deck; and he does so, with his four shadowy companions, when the boats are first lowered for a whale. Contrary to tradition, Captain Ahab orders a spare boat to be lowered for himself and his mysterious crew. The Parsee is a tall, swart figure, clothed in Chinese black but crowned, as it were, with a glistening white turban formed by his living hair braided and coiled round and round upon his head. (The duality of his attire may be indicative of the duality of his Parsee mind.) The other four are there mainly, I suppose, to make a crew for Ahab when his boat is lowered; yet, being necessary, they are turned to symbolic use. They are said to be "less swart in aspect" than the Parsee, being, in fact, of a "vivid, tiger-yellow complexion peculiar to some of the aboriginal natives of the Manillas," a race supposed by "some honest white mariners" to be "the paid spies and secret confidential agents on the water of the devil." I do not think it is pushing the allegorical interpretation too far to see in these four silent yellow savages the primal emotions, just as the Parsee is the primal mind. Together, crew and Parsee represent the whole of Ahab. To their level he has reverted. The oars of these shadowy five rise and fall like trip hammers in perfect unison. They are as responsive to Ahab's will as musicians playing in wild, yet rhythmic, patterns at the behest of their conductor. The somewhat spectral quality of the shadowy five gives the picture the heightened realism of visionary art. It is as if the wall of flesh had been removed from Ahab and his mad mind and his mad passions had been projected into the realm of eternal being. In that realm words are alien, and so it is right that Ahab's words should be withheld. "But what it was that inscrutable Ahab said to that tiger yellow crew of his—these were words best omitted here; for you live under the blessed light of the evangelical land. Only the infidel sharks in the audacious seas may give ear to such words, when with tornado brow, and eyes of red murder, and foam-glued lips, Ahab leaped after his prey."

In Ahab's boat the Parsee is harpooner. He is not, however, an emblem of the passions, as are the harpooners on the "Pequod," but here, as always, the projection of Ahab's mind. Ahab's tired body may go below, but the Parsee never does, nor does he ever sleep. Whenever Ahab is moved to meditation or beset by anxiety, the Parsee shares his thoughts. When the tenor of Ahab's life quickens into drama, the Parsee is almost certain to be there, a silent participant. When death is near, the Parsee goes first, as Ahab's pilot. Thus the seducing reason, the Spectre, the Mephistopheles, who piloted Ahab into his course and determined its direction, pilots him out of it.

VI

In this report the "Pequod" has been very slow in setting out and very slow in getting forward on its journey. I left it with Ahab assuming his crown of defiance and despair. The time was sunset. Three successive scenes, entitled "Dusk," "Night," and "Midnight," carry the "Pequod" into darkness and storm, these being the counterparts in nature of the darkness and violence in the minds of the mates and crew.

First, "Dusk," and, with it, Starbuck. He suffers humiliation. In the presence of his dictator he has been an appeaser. He has good will, but little insight and no backbone. He weighs himself in the balance and finds himself wanting. Then "Night" and, with it, Stubb, who has less insight than Starbuck, nothing but a sense that something ominous is brewing and that it can simply be laughed off. Then "Midnight," the deep darkness and the storm, matched by a crew lacking even in the sense of something ominous, giving all to ill-timed jollity, to the reluctant tambourine of Pip. Poor, sensitive Pip, sensitive to the point of madness, sensitive to the point of wisdom, a spiritual castaway among this crew, he alone preserves in his true heart the fear of God, he alone can bring this orgy to sober judgment:

But there they go, all cursing, and here I don't. Fine prospects to 'em; they're on the road to heaven. Hold on hard! Jimmini, what a squall! . . . Here have I heard all their chat just now, and the white whale—shirr! shirr!—but spoken of once! and only this evening—it makes me jingle all over like my tambourine—that anaconda of an old man swore 'em in to hunt him! Oh, thou big white God aloft there somewhere in yon darkness, have mercy on this small black boy down here; preserve him from all men that have no bowels to feel fear!

Ahab lost no time in celebrating his victory. The mate took over, with orders to "kill a squall, something as they burst a waterspout with a pistol—fire your ship right into it!" thus setting the captain free to begin at once mapping out his strategy. He went down into his cabin, brought out a "large wrinkled roll of yellowish sea charts," and proceeded to study the areas where he might find good hunting.

While thus employed, the heavy pewter lamp suspended in chains over his head, continually rocked with the motion of the ship, and for ever threw shifting gleams and shadows of lines upon his wrinkled brow, till it almost seemed that while he himself was marking out lines and courses on the wrinkled charts, some invisible pencil was also tracing lines and courses upon the deeply marked chart of his forehead.

The emergent plan was to carry on the hunt along the line of the equator:

That particular set time and place were conjoined in the one technical phrase—the Season-on-the-Line. For there and then, for several consecutive years, Moby Dick had been periodically descried, lingering in those waters for awhile, as the sun, in its annual round, loiters for a predicted interval in any one sign of the Zodiac. There it was, too, that most of the deadly encounters with the white whale had taken place; there the waves were storied with his deeds; there also was that tragic spot where the monomaniac old man had found the awful motive to his vengeance.

In a book pervaded, as this one is, by a Swedenborgian apprehension of natural imagery, a book, that is to say, in which nature and the soul of man are linked together "beyond all utterance," the fact of these lines and their correspondences invites interpretation, especially as we are told that this chapter, and specifically this portion of it, is as important as any chapter in the book. It is to be observed, then, that the lines on Ahab's wrinkled brow correspond to the lines on his wrinkled charts; and that the lines upon his forehead are frequently placed (like the lines on the Parsee's hand) in correspondence with the lines on the forehead of Moby Dick. I have already had occasion to notice the lined quality of Ahab's world and the great divide of good and evil encircling it like an equator. Nothing could be more natural, in the language of metaphor, than to say that the great moral battles of the world have been fought along that line, than to make that line the birthplace and the death-place of Ahab's revenge, than to say that a feverish concern with that line and its tributaries would stamp itself in lines upon the brow and upon the hand—the mind's hand—dealing the blow daily and nightly.

But there are still other lines. Captain Ahab has a birthmark, and this, too, has a correspondence in the outward world. In the scene of revelry just mentioned, the Old Manx Sailor says: "Our captain has his birthmark; look yonder, boys, there's another in the sky—lurid-like, ye see, all else pitch black." But the birthmark is also a line:

Threading its way out from among his grey hairs, and continuing right down one side of his tawny scorched face and neck, till it disappeared in his clothing, you saw a slender rod-like mark, lividly whitish. It resembled that perpendicular seam sometimes made in the straight, lofty trunk of a great tree, when the upper lightning tearingly darts down it, and without wrenching a single twig, peels and grooves out the bark from top to bottom, ere running off into the soil, leaving the tree still greenly alive, but branded. Whether that mark was born with him, or whether it was the scar left by some desperate wound, no one could certainly say. By some tacit consent, throughout the voyage little or no allusion was made to it, especially by the mates. But once Tashtego's senior, an old Gay-Head Indian among the crew, superstitiously asserted that not till he was full forty years old did Ahab become that way branded, and then it came upon him, not in the fury of any mortal fray, but in an elemental strife at sea. Yet, this wild hint seemed inferentially negatived, by what a grey Manxman insinuated, an old sepulchral man, who, having never before sailed out of Nantucket, had never ere this laid eye upon wild Ahab. Nevertheless, the old sea-traditions, the immemorial credulities, popularly invested this old Manxman with preternatural powers of discernment. So that no white sailor seriously contradicted him when he said that if ever Captain Ahab should be tranquilly laid out—which might hardly come to pass, so he muttered—then, whoever should do that last office for the dead, would find a birth-mark on him from crown to sole.

The apparent inconsistency between a birthmark and a line that was not drawn for forty years is easily resolved. The birthmark was always there; the line took Ahab's lifetime to run its course. In the terminology of today, the birthmark might be likened to the genes, the line to conditioning.

That is a longitudinal line, but the latitude is also marked upon him; he lives right under the hot equator. Everyone must have said it to himself; it is the Carpenter who speaks out:

"He goes aft. That was sudden, now; but squalls come sudden in hot latitudes. I've heard that the Isle of Albemarle, one of the Gallipagos, is cut by the Equator right in the middle. Seems to me some sort of Equator cuts yon old man, too, right in his middle. He's always under the Line—fiery hot, I tell ye!

The equator cuts Ahab "right in the middle" in yet another way. For there upon the mainmast, which, incidentally, divides the ship in two, is nailed a gold doubloon, a coin of Ecuador, "a country planted in the middle of the world, and beneath the great equator." Ahab nailed it there as he opened the great scene upon the quarter-deck, intending it to be a sign and symbol of the chase and a perpetual reminder of it, lest, in the course of time, the crew forget. For those who could not read its hidden meaning it hung there as a golden reward for whosoever should first sing out, "Moby Dick!" And then, on the first of the last three days, when Ahab had himself earned the reward, he resorted once again to the doubloon to screw their courage to the sticking point, lest it should fail. Meanwhile, it hung there, exerting daily and nightly a mysterious and almost hypnotic influence, a golden prize for someone, yet also a continual, if dim, reminder to the crew that they were under the line—the line that divides good from evil:

> Nor, though placed amongst a ruthless crew and every hour passed by ruthless hands, and through the livelong nights shrouded with thick darkness which might cover any pilfering approach, nevertheless every sunrise found the doubloon where the sunset left it last. For it was set apart and sanctified to one awe-striking end; and however wanton in their sailor ways, one and all, the mariners revered it as the white whale's talisman. Sometimes they talked it over in the weary watch by night, wondering whose it was to be at last, and whether he would ever live to spend it.

Several members of the crew read the doubloon in their several ways, among them the Parsee, who bowed silently before it. He must, for the segment of the Zodiac which bent around the top of the golden coin represented the sun in the sign of Libra. What could this mean except that the Parsee sun was weighing good and evil in the Scales? It is, however, an ominous position. For a time the sun may linger there, but not for long; nothing can hold it back, nothing can keep it from falling into Scorpio—the sign of the scorpion, which, in Greek fable, stung and killed Orion, that mighty hunter. The sign of Libra, again, in relation to the human figure, like the equator in relation to the earth, cuts it "right in the middle." Under this line the mighty hunter who commands the "Pequod" pursues his course.

Finally, we may look for lines in the principal owners of the "Pequod," Captain Bildad and Captain Peleg. Both, it is said, were "fighting Quakers; . . . Quakers with a vengeance." There is one line. But their names take us back to the Old Testament, where we find other suggestions of a divided self. Bildad was one of those friends who vexed the soul of Job with their mockery. False friends they were, insincere and therefore double-minded. Our Bildad outdoes his namesake. He is a hypocrite, a pious fraud. It seems that "he had long since come to the sage and sensible conclusion that a man's religion is one thing, and this practical world quite another. This world pays dividends." The Bible says that one must choose between God and Mammon, that he who is for the one must be against the other. Not so Captain Bildad. He chooses both. Of Peleg the Bible says one thing and only one: that the world was divided in his days. The name itself means "division." It signifies something, therefore, that the two owners have in common. The spirit of division broods double over the ship in which Ahab's divided mind looks out upon a divided world.

Days and weeks passed. The "Pequod" was heading south toward the Cape. The nights were white. Think of Ahab as in his cabin, taking advantage of the night to study his maps and charts, and of the Parsee (his counterpart) as in the crow's nest, scanning the sea as intently as by day, although not one sailor in a hundred would venture to lower for a whale at night. Suddenly, at the midnight hour, far ahead, an apparition—a silvery jet like "some plumed and glittering god uprising from the sea." The Parsee first descried it and with "unearthly voice" broke the silence with the familiar and exciting whaleman's cry, "There she blows!" Ahab got the ship into full speed, but the silvery jet was seen no more. Night after night this happened. At the silent midnight hour the apparition would be again announced, but each and every time it disappeared. "Mysteriously jetted into the clear moon-light, or starlight, as the case might be; disappearing again for one whole day, or two days, or three; and somehow seeming at every distinct repetition to be advancing still further and further in our van, this solitary jet seemed for ever alluring us on."

What Ahab's secret thoughts were in relation to this spectacle we are not told. Did he reflect, as he pursued his course through a wilderness of waters, upon the pillar of fire in which the Lord manifested himself by night to the Israelites wandering in the wilderness? In the great crisis of his life, when the Lord manifested himself in white lights upon the masts, Ahab cried out, defiantly, "The white flame but lights the way to the White Whale!" Whatever Ahab's secret thoughts, the instincts of the crew were sound:

For a time, there reigned, too, a sense of peculiar dread at this flitting apparition, as if it were treacherously beckon-ing us on and on, in order that the monster might turn round upon us, and rend us at last in the remotest and most savage seas.

This is what was actually to happen. Did Ahab never share the dread, in his despairing moods? Or had his deceitful mind (the Parsee) deceived him utterly? Did his thoughts never revert to the story of King Ahab, who was lured to his doom by a lying spirit?

Therefore hear thou the word of the Lord: I saw the Lord sitting on his throne, and all the host of heaven standing by him on his right hand and on his left. And the Lord said, Who shall entice Ahab, that he may go up and fall at Ramoth-gilead? And one said on this manner; and another said on that manner. And there came forth a spirit, and stood before the Lord, and said, I will entice him. And the Lord said unto him, Wherewith? And he said, I will go forth, and will be a lying spirit in the mouth of all his prophets. And he said, Thou shalt entice him, and shalt prevail also: go forth, and do so.

If this suggestion was worth making, it is worth pursuing. It is to be noted, therefore, that the spirit-spout is wholly on the plane of the supernatural, unlike the plausible apparition of the Squid, which follows soon, and that it is first descried by the Parsee, whereas the Squid is descried by Daggoo. And if the Parsee has a luring, diabolical, Mephistophelean quality—which is certain—he stands in distant relationship to the Spirit who entered into the wilderness to try his arts upon the Savior, and who, as Milton tells the story, recalled some previous exploits:

> And when to all his Angels he proposed
> To draw the proud king Ahab into fraud,
> That he might fall in Ramoth, they demurring,
> I undertook that office.

All round the Cape, in all kinds of weather, the solitary jet continued to appear, from time to time, until, having served its purpose, it was descried no more.

The silent, mysterious spirit-spout is succeeded by another silent and mysterious apparition, a returning whaling vessel, appropriately named the "Albatross." The "Pequod" had struggled round the Cape and had encountered howling winds and troubled seas and dismal nights. The ivory-tusked ship gored her way into the dark waves. Along this stretch, as so often, nature and the soul of man are linked beyond all utterance; but once, at least, the linkage is uttered superbly:

> And heaved and heaved, still unrestingly heaved the black sea, as if its vast tides were a conscience; and the great mundane soul were in anguish and remorse for the long sin and suffering it had bred.

In the continual tempest, through which the solitary midnight spirit-spout, like a supernatural warning, could occasionally be descried, Ahab stood almost continually on deck, sunk in the gloomiest reserve. He "more seldom than ever addressed his mates."

In tempestuous times like these, after everything above and aloft has been secured, nothing more can be done but passively to await the issue of the gale. Then Captain and crew become practical fatalists. So, with his ivory leg inserted into its accustomed hole, and with one hand firmly grasping a shroud, Ahab for hours and hours would stand gazing dead to windward, while an occasional squall of sleet or snow would all but congeal his very eyelashes together. . . . Few or no words were spoken; and the silent ship, as if manned by painted sailors in wax, day after day tore on through all the swift madness and gladness of the demoniac waves. By night the same muteness of humanity before the shrieks of the ocean prevailed; still in silence the men swung in the bowlines; still wordless Ahab stood up to the blast.

It is inspired placing that now brings Ahab's silent and almost deathly "Pequod," outgoing, alongside the silent and almost deathly "Albatross," incoming. Like the spirit-spout, like Moby Dick himself, her hue is white, not their brilliant, living, heavenly white but a deathlike pallor:

> As if the waves had been fullers, this craft was bleached like the skeleton of a stranded walrus. All down her sides,

this spectral appearance was traced with long channels of reddened rust, while all her spars and her rigging were like the thick branches of trees furred over with hoar-frost.

Four years she had been cruising, and with what report? Her lookouts, forlorn-looking and mild-eyed fishermen, said not a word to the lookouts of the "Pequod," close to them as they came. But Ahab's voice thundered from the quarter-deck: "Ship ahoy! Have ye seen the White Whale?" This was to be Ahab's imperious question of every incoming captain. But the power of chance, or the power that sent the spirit-spout and fashioned Moby Dick in white, forbade an answer:

But as the strange captain, leaning over the pallid bulwarks, was in the act of putting his trumpet to his mouth, it somehow fell from his hand into the sea; and the wind now rising amain, he in vain strove to make himself heard without it. Meantime his ship was still increasing the distance between. While in various silent ways the seamen of the Pequod were evincing their observance of this ominous incident at the first mere mention of the White Whale's name to another ship, Ahab for a moment paused; it almost seemed as though he would have lowered a boat to board the stranger, had not the threatening wind forbade.

Foiled, he took refuge in self-affirmation. Again he seized his trumpet and cried out:

"Ahoy there! This is the Pequod, bound round the world! Tell them to address all future letters to the Pacific ocean! and this time three years, if I am not at home, tell them to address them to —"

The two wakes crossed, and it happened that shoals of fish that for some days had been swimming placidly beside the "Pequod," "darted away with what seemed shuddering fins, and ranged themselves fore and aft with the stranger's flanks." There is an effort to make this obvious piece of symbolism appear natural; but to Ahab it was an omen:

"Swim away from me, do ye?" murmured Ahab, gazing over into the water. There seemed but little in the words, but the tone conveyed more of deep helpless sadness than the insane old man had ever before evinced.

This is despair; but it is countered immediately by despair-born defiance:

But turning to the steersman, who thus far had been holding the ship in the wind to diminish her headway, he cried out in his old lion voice,—"Up helm! Keep her off round the world!"

Not a word, then, to the sensual ear did Ahab get; but his spirit, had it been receptive, would have heard a message beyond all verbal utterance. The purport of it would have been a warning to stay his vengeful hand. In the deathly whiteness of the "Albatross," as well as in the living whiteness of Moby Dick, there is a union of contraries, a union which includes the moral contraries of good and evil. In that single color they are symbolically held together in a mysterious unity beyond the power of the finite mind to comprehend, and beyond the power of the finite hand to separate and avenge. To a sensitive spirit the message would have defined itself in various ways, among them these:

Be still and know that I am God.—Resist not evil.— For the wrath of man worketh not the righteousness of God.—Vengeance is mine, saith the Lord.

All this and more the apparition says, speaking with the silent and sovereign authority of symbol.

In the course of time there comes a third white apparition, bearing the same message and bearing it unmistakably. It required no intuition to understand, sailors' talk had settled it. One still, transparent morning Daggoo descried in the distance a great white mass which slowly lifted itself from the blue surface of the water, glistened for a moment in the sunlight, and slowly sank down again. Again this happened, and yet again. Could it be the White Whale? Boats were lowered, but the quarry turned out to be, not Moby Dick, but "the most wondrous phenomenon which the secret seas have hitherto revealed to mankind":

A vast pulpy mass, furlongs in length and breadth, of a glancing cream-color, lay floating on the water, innumerable long arms radiating from its centre, and curling and twisting like a nest of anacondas, as if blindly to catch at any hapless object within reach. No perceptible face or front did it have; no conceivable token of either sensation or instinct; but undulated there on the billows, an unearthly, formless, chance-like apparition of life.

It is the great live squid. Flask's incurious mind has never heard of it. Whales he knew about; it was, in fact, his business to destroy them, whenever possible. And yet—

So utterly lost was he to all sense of reverence for the many marvels of their majestic bulk and mystic ways; and so dead to anything like an apprehension of any possible danger from encountering them; that in his poor opinion, the wondrous whale was but a species of magnified mouse, or at least water-rat, requiring only a little circumvention and some small application of time and trouble in order to kill and boil.

Starbuck, on the other hand, was sensitive and intuitive. "Outward portents and inward presentiments were his." Here is a portent, certainly:

As with a low sucking sound it slowly disappeared again, Starbuck still gazing at the agitated waters where it had sunk, with a wild voice exclaimed—"Almost rather had I seen Moby Dick and fought him, than to have seen thee, thou white ghost!"

"What was it, Sir?" said Flask.

"The great live squid, which, they say, few whale-ships ever beheld, and returned to their ports to tell of it."

But Ahab said nothing; turning his boat, he sailed back to the vessel; the rest as silently following.

VII

There are many silences in Ahab's life. They are part of his tragedy, and not the least important part. They are silences that take refuge in morbid seclusion or reserve, silences inclosing dread, the silences of a spirit turned demonic. Silences of this kind, being related to dread and the demonic, to despair and sickness unto death, fell under Kierkegaard's searching eye. The demonic person, he says, becomes more and more shut up and incommunicative. Only unwillingly does he open his lips in speech. So it was with Ahab. Physically and spiritually he made himself as inaccessible as possible. Dinners in the cabin were eaten in "awful silence." It was not that Ahab forbade conversation, only that he himself was dumb. In truth, he was preoccupied with another kind of nourishment. Like the last of the Missouri grizzly bears, which are described as hibernating in the hollow of a tree and sucking their own paws, "Ahab's soul, shut up in the caved trunk of his body, there fed upon the sullen paws of its gloom!" At night, a visitor to the cabin, had there been one, would have found him under the swinging lamp, plotting his course with military zeal and anxiety. Surely, the reader's mind is expected to revert to Jonah, the subject of Father Mapple's sermon. Jonah is described as lying in his lamplit cabin, where the steadfast, though swinging, lamp revealed the "false, lying levels" of the unbalanced ship.

"The lamp alarms and frightens Jonah; as lying in his berth his tormented eyes roll round the place, and this thus far successful fugitive finds no refuge for his restless glance. But that contradiction in the lamp more and more appals him. The floor, the ceiling, and the side, are all awry. 'Oh! so my conscience hangs in me!' he groans, 'straight upward, so it burns; but the chambers of my soul are all in crookedness!' "

Jonah, the Father continues, is "not yet supplicating God for mercy," but this fear of God is the beginning of his deliverance. In Ahab there is no such fear, and therefore no prospect of release. From time to time, when the weather maddens his resistance or the presence of a hunting ground maddens his expectation, Ahab goes into still deeper self-imprisonment. As the "Pequod" fought its way around the Cape, Ahab "more seldom than ever addressed his mates":

Few or no words were spoken; and the silent ship, as if manned by painted sailors in wax, day after day tore on through all the swift madness and gladness of the demoniac waves. By night the same muteness of humanity before the shrieks of the ocean prevailed; still in silence the men swung in the bowlines; still wordless Ahab stood up to the blast.

This is a perfect example of the Kierkegaardian analysis—a sufferer gone mute and surrounded by a wall of incommunication.

But in sleep, even in uneasy sleep, when the waking consciousness is off guard, walls may be breached. Dreams break through, reporting the situation. Sometimes the dream takes the form of pure wish-fulfilment. As Ahab nears those equatorial waters where the evil deed was done and where he intends that it shall be avenged, the eager expectation of the day is satisfied in dreams at night. In his very sleep, "his ringing cry ran through the vaulted hull, 'Stern all! the White Whale spouts thick blood!' "

But there is another dream, oft repeated, in which the neurotic conflict is reflected in anxiety, not resolved in triumph. Even in sleep the battle rages, humanities against inhumanities, if those terms may be accepted; ego against superego, in Freudian terminology. The humanities, which include the voice of conscience, resort to threats of punishment, sometimes opening up a vision of hell itself before Ahab's affrighted eyes. Then "a wild cry would be heard through the ship; and with glaring eyes Ahab would burst from his state room, as though escaping from a bed that was on fire."

Such are the crises of Ahab's demonic temper. More moving, however, more tragic even, are those sudden stabs of thought or feeling, vents of defiance or despair, witnesses to the tension and the torment. The endless asking of the alien seas, the endless asking of the stars and the abysses between the stars, the anxious questions and the mocking answers—these could break the mind, though wind and weather could not break the body.

A mind wearied with the weight of speculation utters its weariness in a soliloquy addressed to the black and hooded head of a decapitated whale, a soliloquy compact of black and hooded thoughts, as spiritless as the intense copper calm which, "like a universal yellow lotus, was more and more unfolding its noiseless measureless leaves upon the sea."

"Sail ho!" cried a triumphant voice from the main-mast-head.

"Aye? Well, now, that's cheering," cried Ahab, suddenly erecting himself, while whole thunder-clouds swept aside from his brow. "That lively cry upon this deadly calm might almost convert a better man.—Where away?"

"Three points on the starboard bow, sir, and bringing down her breeze to us!"

"Better and better, man. Would now St. Paul would come along that way, and to my breezelessness bring his breeze!"

What a long succession of spiritual struggles is condensed in that surprising word "convert" and in that reference to St. Paul, a reference which seems at first sight so odd and so irrelevant. Has Ahab been thinking of the Apostle sailing the Mediterranean with energies so like his own and purposes so different? Have the humanities stung Ahab's memory with many a pointed sentence? "Not I, but Christ in me," have they reminded him, suggesting that "Not I, but the demon in me," would suit his case? Or "Who will deliver me from the body of this death?" All this, no doubt, and more and still more, all wisely left unspecified, since it is all suggested by that single, sudden, despairing cry.

Again, Starbuck goes down into the cabin to report that the oil in the hold is leaking. But Ahab's thoughts are on his charts, on Moby Dick, and on himself:

"Begone! Let it leak! I'm all aleak myself. Aye! leaks in leaks! not only full of leaky casks, but those leaky casks are in a leaky ship; and that's a far worse plight than the Pequod's, man. Yet I don't stop to plug my leak; for who can find it in the deep-loaded hull; or how hope to plug it, even if found, in this life's howling gale?"

Somehow, without being imitative, that suggests *Macbeth*, and so, still more, does a colloquy with the blacksmith:

"Look ye here, then," cried Ahab, passionately advancing, and leaning with both hands on Perth's shoulders; "look ye here—*here*—can ye smooth out a seam like this, blacksmith," sweeping one hand across his ribbed brow; "if thou could'st, blacksmith, glad enough would I lay my head upon thy anvil, and feel thy heaviest hammer between my eyes. Answer! Can'st thou smooth this seam?"

Ahab had to learn, as Macbeth did, that this is a condition wherein the patient must minister to himself, and, like Macbeth, he scorns self-ministration.

This scene with the blacksmith is intense. It must be, since Ahab is preparing to pile blasphemy on blasphemy by tempering (or baptizing) his newly forged branding-iron in human heathen blood. The blacksmith's forge provides a background of fire—fire not light, fire in correspondence with Ahab's fiery will and with the fiery hell in Ahab's mind. The blacksmith has suffered too, physically and mentally; he has, so to speak, been scorched all over, so that he is proof against the sparks of fire flying from his anvil. But immunity from the fret and fever of the world seems to Ahab an evasion, even a misfortune. The blacksmith should be mad, like himself; it is the right adjustment to a tormented world. Ahab's bitterness approaches Swift's:

"Thy shrunk voice sounds too calmly, sanely woful to me. In no Paradise myself, I am impatient of all misery in others that is not mad. Thou should'st go mad, black-smith; say, why dost thou not go mad? Do the heavens yet hate thee, that thou can'st not go mad?"

The carpenter, like the blacksmith, pierces Ahab's defenses. Both of them do it, not wilfully or even consciously, but like the gravediggers in *Hamlet*, by turning up, in the simple pursuit of their vocations, occasions that break through. A chapter entitled "Ahab and the Carpenter" shows the carpenter in the foreground, fashioning a new leg for Ahab, a joist of ivory in his vise, and the blacksmith in the background working at his forge. The despairing mood is uppermost in Ahab. Let the blacksmith be directed "to forge a pair of steel shoulderblades; there's a pedlar aboard with a crushing pack." In his dejection the red fires of the forge suggest, through a rapid round of associations, that "hell's probable."

Waking or asleep, hell threatens. It is not merely a future threat, it is a present reality. Ahab does not say precisely, "Myself am hell," as Satan does, but word and deed imply it. The thought here begun in relation to the blacksmith is concluded in relation to the carpenter. The conclusion is that one may "feel the fiery pains of hell for ever, and without a body," just as Ahab still feels pain in his lost leg.

The pains of hell in the soul may turn pain of any kind into a kind of pleasure. Ahab turns the vise against his fingers until the carpenter cries out, not Ahab. The pleasure of the pain is that he likes "to feel something in this slippery world that can hold."

What a vista of suffering that need opens up! For it is really a spiritual hold that Ahab wants, and this is a confession that he hasn't found it. From those secret sessions with the Parsee just subsequent to sailing, to the present colloquies with the blacksmith and the carpenter, there has been no peace, only continual conflict between the Parsee, rationalizing revenge, and the humanities, undoing every argument.

The question comes to mind, What kind of man could hold his stance? Ahab orders such a one, as he fancies him. He is to be fifty feet high and the rest proportionately. Two specifications tap Ahab's inmost thoughts. This man of "desirable pattern" is to have "no heart at all." The prohibition reveals incalculable suffering. The suffering might be mitigated if the heart but knew. "A quarter of an acre of fine brains" would help. And then, "Let me see—shall I order eyes to see outwards?" No, not outward-seeing eyes. The endless asking, the daily and nightly scrutiny of sea and sky, have brought no satisfying answer. "No, but put a skylight on top of his head to illuminate inwards." Inward illumination would show the way, certainly; but there is no light from the dark fires raging within Ahab, no light at all. His head is a "blind dome." It is a confession, for the moment, of complete despair. Perhaps the plight of Diogenes occurs to him. Anyway, in the absence of outward and inward light, he "must have a lantern." The carpenter offers him one. Mockery caps despair.

Presently, however, the defiant mood returns, to re-create the conflict. "Oh, Life! Here I am, proud as Greek god, and yet standing debtor to this blockhead for a bone to stand on! Cursed be that mortal inter-indebtedness which will not do away with ledgers." This is one aspect of the problem which arises from willing, in despair, to be one's self. The problem is insoluble by any light that Ahab has, outward or inward.

VIII

Thus a flash of light from time to time illuminates the depths of Ahab's soul and reminds us that there is never an hour's respite from the crushing pack. Upon the crew, however, Ahab found it advisable to practice some dissimulation. Shrewdly aware that he had done a dangerous thing in altering the purpose of the voyage and that a crew of sordid men could not indefinitely maintain an oath taken under excitement and enchantment, he "plainly saw that he must still in a good degree continue true to the natural, nominal purpose of the Pequod's voyage" and "observe all customary usages." To some readers these "customary usages," yes, even the disquisitions in cetology, might have overtones of meaning, since, to quote the text, "some certain significance lurks in all things, else all things are little worth." But I hope not to cross the line which separates interpretation from mere revery. Even Ishmael is conscious of such a line. He is unable, he admits, to dive into the minds of the ordinary members of the crew and say what Ahab's strange purposes meant to them. My line is much closer in than Ishmael's, but I believe that it admits the returning ships.

One—the "Albatross"—has already come and gone. Another was coming when the cry "Sail ho!" was heard in the deadly calm, and Ahab wished it would bring St. Paul and his breeze to his own breezelessness. The wish was not fulfilled. The ship, significantly named the "Jeroboam," carries a mad prophet bearing no discernible relation to St. Paul and bringing no breeze to inspirit Ahab.

The "Albatross," it will be remembered, a silent apparition appareled in the mystery of white, said silently: "Thou shalt not" and, more specifically, "Thou shalt not set up other gods before me." But this is what Jeroboam did. He set up images of other gods and burned incense at their altars, being opposed in all this by a prophet. Now, when Ahab came to the throne, he walked in Jeroboam's sins, setting up altars to false gods and being opposed, in his turn, by a still greater prophet (Elijah). Is it not to be supposed that Captain Ahab would be struck by the fact that the name of this approaching vessel is the "Jeroboam" and that a mad prophet (Gabriel) is on board, a prophet of the Shaker sect, proclaiming that the White Whale is sacred and inviolable, being, in fact, the Shaker God incarnated? It is learned that, when the "Jeroboam" sighted Moby Dick, the first mate (Macey) lowered for the attack, in spite of Gabriel's protestations; but, as he stood with poised lance, he was suddenly thrown out of the boat with such force that he made a long arc in his descent and sank at a distance of about fifty yards. (Something very like this was to happen when the "Pequod" first entered Moby Dick's home territory.) "Think, think of the blasphemer," exclaimed Gabriel to Ahab, pointing downward, "dead, and down there!—beware of the blasphemer's end!" As if this were not enough, it turns out that there is a letter on board the "Pequod" for someone on board the "Jeroboam"—the dead Macey, as it happens. "Nay, keep it thyself," cried Gabriel to Ahab; "thou art soon going that way." But Ahab is as contemptuous of prophets as his biblical namesake and as Jeroboam. Cursing him, he tries to deliver the letter, but Gabriel contrives to send it back, and it falls at Ahab's feet. This is plain speaking on the part of Providence, for it says, in its way, what Elijah said to King Ahab: "And I will make thine house like the house of Jeroboam"—a prophecy of destruction. True, the full-length incident includes details which might have tended to confuse the message, but the source of confusion, if there was any, was Ahab's wilfulness. The common seamen caught the drift, so that "many strange things" were hinted among them in reference to "this wild affair."

Weeks pass, and one event succeeds another, some with a secondary meaning, implicit or explicit, others merely factual. Ishmael and Queequeg become involved in an incident wherein they seem like twin brothers. Queequeg is down in the sea, on the back of a whale, in fact, and tied to one end of a rope, while Ishmael is tied to the other end. Two lives and one fate, Ishmael reflected; even setting aside a fatal outcome, he felt that his own individuality "was now merged in a joint stock company of two." Queequeg escaped all danger, including the devouring sharks; his time had not yet come. All this, in due course, will be seen to have deep significance. Tashtego also narrowly escaped death. His time also had not yet come. He was destined to go down with the "Pequod," proudly nailing the flag to the mainmast of the sinking ship. And then, after these and other incidents, comes a ship oddly named the "Virgin"; and then again, after a suitable interval, which can be silently passed over, comes the "Rose-Bud."

The captain of the "Jeroboam" had heard of Moby Dick, had even seen him; but the captains of the "Virgin" and the "Rose-Bud" know and care nothing about that matter. Captain Derick, of the "Virgin," is merely seeking oil, oil for the lamps of Holland. Almost unbelievably, he has no oil for his own lamps and stands begging. The ship is said to deserve its name of "Virgin" by reason of this emptiness, but the parable inevitably comes to mind. Unlike the foolish virgins, who asked for oil, Captain Derick gets some, but he hasn't common sense enough to keep it safe. The captain of the "Virgin" is indeed a very foolish captain. He entered into a contest with Stubb and the other two mates for an old and ailing whale which Stubb and his companions had caught, but alas! it sank. Having lost that contest, Captain Derick proceeded to lose another, going in chase of an uncapturable Fin-Back, which he mistook for a Sperm. "Oh! many are the Fin-Backs, and many are the Dericks, my friend." So the chapter concludes, meaning, possibly, that deceived and deceivers are plentiful in this world. And many, it might have added, are the whales that sink. More important, perhaps, than this is the fact that, as soon as Captain Derick evinced his complete ignorance of the White Whale, Captain Ahab evinced complete uninterest in him. What shall we say? That some are beset by the problem of good and evil, while others are unaware of its existence, and that neither party has any interest in the other?

The "Rose-Bud" also is not on a white chase. Very

likely it's seeking oil. What turns up is ambergris, suspected by Stubb and secured by "unrighteous cunning." The French captain is tricked into pulling away from the stinking whale, which, however, like the toad, ugly and venomous, bears precious ambergris near its fin. This whole episode, including a delightful bit of comedy, is of no interest to Ahab; it only stirs him to impatience. Had they seen the White Whale? "Never heard of such a whale. Cachelot Blanche! White Whale —no." That ends it for Ahab. Perhaps the allegorical purpose of this chapter is only to set off Ahab once more in his lonely isolation from his fellows, whether cunning or simple. If one wished to go further, one might say that, in this mysterious mass of suffering called "evil," there is hidden a precious good. The Ahabs cannot find this good, being blinded to it by their sensitity to evil. The French captains cannot find even the worldly good they seek, not being wise in the world's ways. But the Stubbs succeed. They are in the world and of the world, and have the cunning to collect the world's dividends.

The comic is succeeded by the tragic. A few days after the encounter with the Rose-Bud, poor black Pip, he of the tambourine, he of the tender heart, almost lost his life and did lose his wits. He was left alone—abandoned—on the sea, a whale being more important. It was by mere chance that he was rescued. Yet the whale, purchased at the price of Pip's sanity, yielded a great quantity of sperm. Together, the sailors went to work upon it, and the work was such a sweet, fragrant, and fraternal an occupation that Ishmael forgot the horrible Oath, forgot all feelings of ill-will, and became conscious of no feeling except fellowship. He enjoyed an almost mystical experience:

> Would that I could keep squeezing that sperm for ever! For now, since by many prolonged, repeated experiences, I have perceived that in all cases man must eventually lower, or at least shift, his conceit of attainable felicity; not placing it anywhere in the intellect or the fancy; but in the wife, the heart, the bed, the table, the saddle, the fire-side, the country; now that I have perceived all this, I am ready to squeeze case eternally. In thoughts of the visions of the night, I saw long rows of angels in paradise, each with his hands in a jar of spermaceti.

But this vision of the night was followed by another vision, also of the night, but reality, not dream. The blubber was thrown into the try-works, where the Leviathan burned by his own fuel:

> Would that he consumed his own smoke! for his smoke is horrible to inhale, and inhale it you must, and not only that, but you must live in it for the time. It has an unspeakable, wild, Hindoo odor about it, such as may lurk in the vicinity of funereal pyres. It smells like the left wing of the day of judgment; it is an argument for the pit.

The sight and smell evoke another dream-vision, hell-ish, not heavenly. Ishmael dreamed he was at the tiller but had somehow turned himself around and was facing backward. He righted himself just in time to prevent capsizing. Out of the same sperm, as out of the same world, come visions of heaven and hell.

But in a material way, out of the sperm comes oil; and, before the mess is cleaned up from one capture, three men at three mastheads are scanning the sea for another.

And now it is time for another ship. It is the "Samuel

Enderby"—another ship, another captain, another grievous encounter with Moby Dick, another way of taking it. Captain Bonner has lost an arm and has replaced it with a piece of ivory as carefully turned out as Ahab's. There they sit—the two dismasted captains, the silent Parsee, the loquacious doctor. Vengeance? No, might lose another arm. One lowering for that fellow is enough. He's a relative of Stubb, this captain:

". . . he's best let alone; don't you think so, Captain?"—glancing at the ivory leg.

"He is. But he will still be hunted, for all that. What is best let alone, that accursed thing is not always what least allures."

"He is." Two words from the good, wise angel; but immediately the evil angel breaks in, inflaming the passions, whispering of a psychic drive that is irresistible. The blood boils in Ahab's veins; his pulses pound. The good-natured doctor is dumbfounded. "Is your captain crazy?" he asks the Parsee. There is not time for an answer. Ahab's off to head east, where Moby Dick has been reported.

The "Pequod" speeds eastward without, for a time, recorded incident. There are readings in cetology. Now it is that Ahab orders a new leg from the carpenter, and from the blacksmith a new harpoon. At last the Pacific opens up before them. For Ishmael the arrival in these waters was an answer to the long supplication of his youth. If he undertook this journey, as he did, to be reconciled to the world, here surely was the place of reconciliation. For here he stood at the center of all the seas, with sweet influences pouring in upon him from sea and air and sky. Overcome, he bowed his head to Pan. Here, too, Starbuck's faith momentarily was deepened, and Stubb's jollity took on new brilliance. Even Ahab responded, but not deeply and not long. His thoughts were less upon the reconciling sea than upon its great white occupant, with whom there could be no reconciliation. Therefore, the demon within him became still more repressive and demonic. "Like an iron statue," Ahab stood at his accustomed place, in desperate vigil.

In contrast with Ahab's demonic self-imprisonment and incommunication and in keeping with the tranquilizing beauty of the Pacific, there comes another ship, a Nantucket ship, homeward bound, and appropriately named the "Bachelor." It is loaded with oil like a whaleman's dream, colors flying everywhere, sailors dancing with Polynesian girls to music issuing from glittering fiddle bows made from ivory of the beloved whale. Will the "Pequod" 's captain accept the invitation of the "Bachelor" 's captain to come aboard and have a drink? He will not. Has the "Bachelor" 's captain seen the White Whale? "No, only heard of him; don't believe in him at all." The spoils of the world seem to go to the children of the world. There lies the point. Ahab is seeking other spoil and has to make a deep renunciation. Not only the "Bachelor" 's rewards, but richer ones—the wife, the child, the peace of mind.

And as Ahab, leaning over the taffrail, eyed the homeward-bound craft, he took from his pocket a small vial of sand, and then looking from the ship to the vial, seemed thereby bringing two remote associations together, for that vial was filled with Nantucket soundings.

Whether his reflections cost him a sigh of remorse or only a sigh of satisfaction over his lonely eminence, we are not told.

It would seem as if whales pursued the "Bachelor." The very next day four were found and slain, one of them by Ahab. He drew his boat apart to watch the sinking sun and the sinking whale expire together. For there is something strange and moving in the last act of an expiring whale—it turns its head sunward as it sinks. Dying, this Leviathan of the sea, this fierce creature in which (when it is Moby Dick) Ahab can see the summation of the world's wrong—dying, it salutes its master, the principle of light and fire and good, and then it sinks to the dark depths of the sea. Often before had Ahab observed it, but the lovely sunset sea and sky, contrasting with the gloom of Ahab's mind, gave this symbolic action a significance, a "wondrousness," not realized before:

"He too worships fire; most faithful, broad, baronial vassal of the sun! . . . here, too, life dies sunwards full of faith; but see! no sooner dead, than death whirls round the corpse, and it heads some other way."

There, once more, is the riddle of a dual world. God made the world, according to the Koran, not for a toy, but in order to render manifest the absolute contrast between good and evil. A cool mind may contemplate such a world with resignation or even with amusement; a believing, fatalistic oriental mind may contemplate it reverently; but a self-willed and passionate mind like Ahab's will have one world, not two; it will be forced to decide whether the evil is less or more real than the good. One might think that the whale's dying homage to the sun would suggest to Ahab the supremacy of light and good, but he makes the other choice. He has surely said to himself already what he says to the carpenter a little later: "So far gone am I in the dark side of earth, that its other side, the theoretic bright one, seems but uncertain twilight to me." And so it is the dying, not the living, whale that speaks to Ahab's spirit:

"Oh, thou dark Hindoo half of nature, who of drowned bones hast builded thy separate throne somewhere in the heart of these unverdured seas; thou art an infidel, thou queen, and too truly speakest to me in the wide-slaughtering Typhoon, and the hushed burial of its after calm."

The dark Hindu half of nature is, I suppose, the world of suffering of which the Hindus were so conscious and from which Buddha found the path of escape. The queen is Isis or Astarte or some similar figure (of which the ancient world had several), an infidel queen, too, having no more faith than Ahab in life and its brief enterprises. Why should she have faith in life—she, the womb and tomb of all? To her, rather than to the sun-god, Ahab's spirit turns with pride in its rejection of illusion, its acceptance of bitter truth. "Nor has this thy whale [Ahab continues] sunwards turned his dying head, and then gone round again, without a lesson to me." The lesson is that all human aspirations, of which the whale's aspiring jet is a symbol, are unavailing. It is in the "darker half," the bitter sea, whose waves are condensed from the breaths of once living things, that Ahab finds comfort for his soul:

"In vain, oh whale, dost thou seek intercedings with yon all-quickening sun, that only calls forth life, but gives it not again. Yet dost thou, darker half, rock me with a prouder, if a darker faith. All thy unnamable imminglings float beneath me here; I am buoyed by breaths of once living things, exhaled as air, but water now.

"Then hail, for ever hail, O sea, in whose eternal tossings the wild fowl finds his only rest. Born of earth, yet suckled by the sea; though hill and valley mothered me, ye billows are my foster-brothers!"

This choice of the "darker half" is the dark doorway to Ahab's fate. Long ago he came to the conclusion that the very ground of the universe was woven in grief and sorrow and that joy, by contrast, was scant and superficial and illusory. "Both the ancestry and posterity of Grief," he thought, "go further than the ancestry and posterity of Joy." Therefore, in his thinking, "even the highest earthly felicities ever have a certain unsignifying pettiness lurking in them," whereas "all heart-woes" have, at bottom, "a mystic significance, and, in some men, an archangelic grandeur." And this is because the children of men, in their sorrows, are children of the gods. For "we must needs give in to this: that the gods themselves are not for ever glad. The ineffaceable, sad birth-mark in the brow of man, is but the stamp of sorrow in the signers." Doubtless Ahab was thinking of the ineffaceable, sad birthmark on his own brow, now drawn into a full-length line. His consolation was that suffering deepened his nature, possessed a mystic significance, and (dare one say?) touched him with archangelic grandeur. His increasing loneliness above and below deck and his increasing torment, of both head and heart, remind one of the trials and sufferings of certain mystics, and all the more so because his participation with the night side of life is nothing less than mystical. But the mystics finally throw their burden off; they emerge out of their dark night into the light, saying that all is or shall be well. Ahab, however, is imprisoned in the stage of suffering. And so the line divides him in still another way. In his calmer moments he can console himself with the worship of the queen whose dwelling is the darker half; but, when the sleeping demon wakes, the Furies take possession.

But Ahab's prouder, darker faith gives short-lived comfort. That very night his dreams delivered him to anxiety. He had been sleeping in his lowered boat, far to windward of the "Pequod," beside a whale that he had killed. Here was a situation cunningly contrived to stir him to the extremity of hope and fear. The hopes and fears are unexpressed but easily imagined. Would that the dead whale were Moby Dick! Yes, but the dead body might be Ahab's—ought to be Ahab's, the voice of conscience said. The dream struggle awakened him, and, awaking, he found himself face to face with the Parsee.

"I have dreamed it again," said Ahab. "Again"—there is an indication of a continuing crisis, a prolonged despair, out of which the defiance of the afternoon rose but momentarily and sank back again. The dream has been of hearses. Half of Ahab's mind, the half that has told him from the first that he is mad, the half that includes his conscience and his intuition—that half has pronounced the sentence of death upon him. But the other half, the proud, passionate, cunning half, seeks annulment or escape. Whenever passion begins to spin the plot, the rationalizing reason is ready to guide it to a tragic outcome. Deceitful justification of a course unjustifiable, deceitful promises of success, deceitful pledges of security—this is the pattern of many a tragic page. To provide false security at this point is the function of the Parsee. Hearses? A hearse with plumes? Let Ahab not be concerned. Two hearses, very strange ones, he must see ere he can die, sights as incredible as that Birnam wood should come to Dunsinane. A second pledge: The Parsee must go first, and, before Ahab can follow, the Parsee must reappear, to be his pilot. Is the implied security merely in the going and returning, or does it lie in some half-conscious supposition that the Parsee, more spirit than flesh, old as Ahab and yet age-less, is a being not born for death? A final pledge: "Hemp only can kill thee." Here is an implied security that frees him from all care:

> "The gallows, ye mean.—I am immortal then, on land and on sea," cried Ahab, with a laugh of derision;—"Immortal on land and on sea!"

The laugh of derision is hysterical. In Ahab's mind the light of reason and the criteria of truth have been ex-tinguished. He has been delivered over to illusions. Macbeth also was taken in by false assurances, but honest Banquo was not deceived:

> And oftentimes, to win us to our harm,
> The instruments of darkness tell us truths,
> Win us with honest trifles, to betray's
> In deepest consequence.

If Ahab's better nature uttered a warning similar to this, he paid as little attention to it as Macbeth. The Parsee's cunning had prevailed.

The Parsee's promises, like the witches' promises, all come true in a way—a mocking, preposterous way. But the artifice of plot is the realism of human nature, since there seems to be no limit to self-deception. Sometimes it seems as if a Lying Spirit were abroad, roaming up and down, seeking whom it may enter into and devour. Mephistopheles knows of such a spirit, whether it be himself or another:

> Let but the Lying Spirit bind thee
> With magic works and shows that blind thee,
> And I shall have thee fast and sure!

But the Lying Spirit cannot enter in unless the door is open. What opens the door? Faust, as Kierkegaard understood him, was personified doubt; and I have already expressed the opinion that doubt was the spirit that entered into Ahab's mind, as he contemplated the duality of good and evil. Mephistopheles says of himself: "I am the spirit that denies." Doubt, denial, deceit —these are involved in one another; they stand in a family relationship. As doubt and denial, the evil spirit tempted Eve; as denial, it got permission to try Job; as doubt, it entered into King Ahab, and, as deceit, it lured him to his death at Ramoth-Gilead. As doubt (if Kierkegaard is right), it entered into Faust; and as doubt, engendering denial and deceit, it entered into the mind of Ahab. Of this seducing spirit the Parsee is the temporary vehicle; but, since this spirit is also resident in the mind of Ahab, it can be said, when the two finish their colloquy, that both become silent, "as one man."

The mysterious and sinister character of the Parsee is recognized by Stubb. He expatiates upon the subject with Flask, who has just enough sense to keep the conversation going. Stubb takes the Parsee to be the "devil in disguise," a conventional devil, with a tail:

"But now, tell me, Stubb, do you suppose that that devil you was speaking of just now, was the same you say is now on board the Pequod?"

"Am I the same man that helped kill this whale? Doesn't the devil live for ever; who ever heard that the devil was dead? Did you ever see any parson a wearing mourning for the devil? And if the devil has a latch-key to get into the admiral's cabin, don't you suppose he can crawl into a port-hole? Tell me that, Mr. Flask?"

The answer, reduced to a sentence, is that his age is beyond computation. It might be said, though Stubb doesn't say it exactly, that he's as old as time, as old as doubt, as old as the father of lies. There is something tricky, something Mephistophelean, about Fedallah. Maybe he'll surrender Moby Dick to Ahab for "his silver watch, or his soul, or something of that sort." Maybe he has "signed a bond" with the old man, maybe he intends to kidnap him. The chapter concludes on a more solemn note. The Parsee

. . . was calmly eyeing the right whale's head, and ever and anon glancing from the deep wrinkles there to the lines in his own hand. And Ahab chanced so to stand, that the Parsee occupied his shadow; while, if the Parsee's shadow was there at all it seemed only to blend with, and lengthen Ahab's.

Once more, they are as one man or, if two men, one shadow.

The Parsee is likely to turn up whenever Ahab's mind is in a state of agitation. Prior to the dream collo-quy there is a scene, already mentioned, in which Ahab has a new harpoon forged and "baptized" in the blood of his three heathen harpooners. As Ahab stood beside the flaming forge, welding his own harpoon, preparing it for a heathen baptism, "the Parsee passed silently, and bowing over his head towards the fire, seemed in-voking some curse or some blessing on the toil." The blessing was upon the work, which furthered the Parsee's purpose; the curse was upon the worker, who was to be its victim. Were the Parsee not there to dramatize the situation, one would say that Ahab's blasphemous mind pronounced a blessing upon the blasphemous procedure, but at the same time it automatically invoked a curse upon himself, the blasphemer.

Ahab and the Parsee coming together as one man means that the part of Ahab's mind which works in doubt and breeds denial and deceit has triumphed. In succession they have been separate and together ever since the relationship began. But in the dream colloquy there is such a deep commitment to deceit that, short of a miracle, it is final. In that submission to the Parsee the light of Ahab's mind went out. Thenceforward, pride and passion rush darkly on, like rapids racing to a fall, leaping over the stones of hindrance which chance or Providence puts in the way.

IX

First in this final sequence of events is the breaking of the quadrant. The "Pequod" had reached equatorial waters and equatorial skies. It was encountering days when "the sky looks lacquered; clouds there are none; the horizon floats; and this nakedness of unrelieved radiance is as the insufferable splendors of God's throne." On such a day it was that Ahab was to declare, in effect, "Let there be no light!"

Ahab waited carefully for the sun to reach its meridian and then brought his quadrant into play in order to take his reading and calculate his latitude. At the same time, the Parsee "was kneeling beneath him on the ship's deck, and with face thrown up like Ahab's, was eyeing the same sun with him; only the lids of his eyes half hooded their orbs, and his wild face was subdued to an earthly passionlessness." Again Ahab and the Parsee are as one man, except that the Parsee, with oriental resignation, calmly awaits the fate which he foresees, whereas Ahab is about to be possessed by Furies.

He calculates his latitude, but the information fails to satisfy. It isn't his own position that he wants to know, it is Moby Dick's. This knowledge the sun must have as it gazes down on the great expanse of waters; but this knowledge it will not give. Of what use is the quadrant? It is a futile instrument, a "foolish toy":

> "Curse thee, thou vain toy; and cursed be all the things that cast man's eyes aloft to that heaven, whose live vividness but scorches him, as these old eyes are even now scorched with thy light, O sun!"

Ahab does not realize that his own inward light has regressed to fire, the consuming fire of passion, and that, by the law of correspondence, the outward light, the sun, must undergo a similar regression and scorch his anxious eyes. Like the good Persian that he says he long has been, he had once worshiped the sun, as being the light of the world, physically and spiritually. For many months, however, he has been looking upon it with an increasingly doubtful eye. There is danger in such speculation. "We boast our light," wrote Milton in the *Areopagitica*, "but if we look not wisely on the sun itself, it smites us into darkness." Ahab is so smitten when he demands of the sun that it light him on his way to his revenge. That white radiance, likened to "the insufferable splendors of God's throne," is beyond good and evil. It is not at the service of man's selfish will.

The light of Ahab's eye having turned to darkness, it is by darkness that he wills to live:

"Level by nature to this earth's horizon are the glances of man's eyes; not shot from the crown of his head, as if God had meant him to gaze on his firmament. Curse thee, thou quadrant!" dashing it to the deck, "no longer will I guide my earthly way by thee; the level ship's compass, and the level dead reckoning, by log and by line; *these* shall conduct me, and show me my place on the sea. Aye," lighting from the boat to the deck, "thus I trample on thee, thou paltry thing that feebly pointest on high; thus I split and destroy thee!"

It is a terrible curse. In demonic pride Ahab abases himself. There is a striking parallel, however, in the curse which Faust places on the moral order. The curse covers a whole complex of aspiration, and concludes:

> Cursed Love's supreme, delicious thrall!
> A curse on Hoping! on Believing!
> And cursed be Patience most of all!

Whereupon a chorus of Spirits exclaims:

> Woe! woe!
> Thou hast it destroyed,
> The beautiful world,
> With powerful fist;
> In ruin 'tis hurled,
> By the blow of a demigod shattered!

The choral comment on Ahab's curse is passed by a single character, and passed silently:

As the frantic old man thus spoke and thus trampled with his live and dead feet, a sneering triumph that seemed meant for Ahab, and a fatalistic despair that seemed meant for himself—these passed over the mute, motionless Parsee's face.

The sneering triumph that passed over the Parsee's face is the triumphant conclusion of the train of deceit set in motion when Ahab imposed the oath of vengeance upon his crew. As the oath was taken, a low laugh was heard from the hold, where the Parsee was still hidden. There the trap was baited, here it's sprung. Along with the triumph, however, there is despair; for the Parsee knows that he is fated to pay the price, along with Ahab. Starbuck and Stubb, the only sensitive souls among the crew, have an intuition of the impending fate. Starbuck comments:

"I have sat before the dense coal fire and watched it all aglow, full of its tormenting flaming life; and I have seen it wane at last, down, down, to dumbest dust. Old man of oceans! of all this fiery life of thine, what will at length remain but one little heap of ashes!"
"Aye," cried Stubb, "but sea-coal ashes—mind ye that, Mr. Starbuck—sea-coal, not your common charcoal."

Ahab, having renounced the light and cursed everything that looks toward heaven, might now be expected to roll darkling down the torrent of his fate. He does; but not without a solemn and magnificent interposition.

When Ahab smashed the quadrant, it was high noon. In a few hours a typhoon struck. Night came, and the sky roared and split with thunder and blazed with lightning. The gale came from the eastward, as if to stop the "Pequod" in her course. The sea stove Ahab's boat. Suddenly, in an interval of profound darkness, all the yardarms were tipped with pallid fire; and the three tall masts were burning "like three gigantic wax tapers before the altar." The corposants! By the sailors of the "Pequod," as by all sailors, those fires were looked upon as "God's burning finger," and in that presence their irreverent tongues were silenced. Even Stubb's gamboling tongue composed itself. "The corpusants have mercy on us all," he cried.

While this pallidness was burning aloft, few words were heard from the enchanted crew; who in one thick cluster stood on the forecastle, all their eyes gleaming in that pale phosphorescence, like a far away constellation of stars. Relieved against the ghostly light, the gigantic jet negro, Daggoo, loomed up to thrice his real stature, and seemed the black cloud from which the thunder had come. The parted mouth of Tashtego revealed his shark-white teeth, which strangely gleamed as if they too had been tipped by corpusants; while lit up by the preternatural light, Queequeg's tattooing burned like Satanic blue flames on his body.

The pallid fires went out, the tableau vanished. But, in a few moments—again the corposants! This time there seemed to be a "redoubled supernaturalness" in their pallor:

At the base of the mainmast, full beneath the doubloon and the flame, the Parsee was kneeling in Ahab's front, but with his head bowed away from him; while near by, from the arched and over-hanging rigging, where they had just been engaged securing a spar, a number of the seamen, arrested by the glare, now cohered together, and hung pendulous, like a knot of numbed wasps from a drooping, orchard twig. In various enchanted attitudes, like the standing, or stepping, or running skeletons in Herculaneum, others remained rooted to the deck; but all their eyes upcast.

It is no accident that these two tableaus throw the harpooners and the Parsee successively into prominence— the harpooners, who represent Ahab's angry passions and in whose blood his harpoon has been baptized not long ago, in the devil's name; and then the Parsee, who represents his mind, a mind initially beset by doubt and now smitten into darkness. Nor is it accidental that these two tableaus should be succeeded by a third, in which Ahab is the central figure:

"Aye, aye, men!" cried Ahab. "Look up at it; mark it well; the white flame but lights the way to the White Whale! Hand me those main-mast links there; I would fain feel this pulse, and let mine beat against it; blood against fire! So."

Then turning—the last link held fast in his left hand, he put his foot upon the Parsee; and with fixed upward eye, and high-flung right arm, he stood erect before the lofty tri-pointed trinity of flames.

The flames are God speaking out of the whirlwind to Ahab, even as he spoke to Job. The sailors on the "Pequod" would no more deny that this "clear spirit of clear fire" is God's burning finger laid upon that ship than they would deny the whirlwind raging round it. Ahab himself acknowledges the fire as his Creator; yet his only answer is defiance. As the nine fires mount to thrice their previous height and declare the glory of God with such overpowering intensity that all the crew, including Ahab, have to lay their hands across their eyes, Ahab's defiance mounts to a comparable height. The speech in which, with darkened eyes his darkened mind finds utterance is one in which this Nantucket sailor, who might at most, one would suppose, aspire to a place alongside Pym and Hampden and Andrew Jackson, can also claim a place alongside Satan and Prometheus. The mind is darkened, truly, and the will is mad with self-assertion; yet the repressed humanities struggle through, and Ahab, at this great moment, is a noble and tragic figure. The intellectual drive here comes to a climax; for once, it dominates the selfish drive, so that Ahab becomes more champion than avenger. As he faces the corposants, unshaken and implacable, he fulfils Captain Peleg's description of him—"an ungodly, godlike man," godlike, or demi-godlike, surely, in his defiance of tyranny in heaven. Admitting the omnipotence of the heavenly light—its "speechless, placeless power"—he bids it strike: "Thou canst consume, but I can then be ashes."

In these words and in the speech of which they are a part, the analogy with the Book of Job continues. The very words just quoted—how like they are to Job's:

> Behold he will slay me; I have no hope.
> Nevertheless I will maintain my ways before him.

A recent study of the Book of Job, attempting to isolate the original poem from extraneous elements, says:

The theme of the poem of Job is the revolt of a suffering, helpless man against a pitiless and all-powerful God. Job has been driven to question the justice and fair-dealing of the Almighty. His own unmerited suffering has opened his eyes to the prevailing misgovernment of the world. God does not rule, as he ought, for the benefit of men, still less does he dispense to each the fortune he deserves. Job stands for the human race in his protest against the evils of human life.

This is precisely how Ahab would like to think of his own protest. But in Ahab's protest righteousness is more than matched by self-righteousness. This is the danger in a moral crisis. A person or a party or a nation may come to believe that the issue is sharply between good and evil. Seen thus, the situation invites to warfare. It is a dangerous invitation, for self-righteousness is itself an evil and a mask for many other evils. The "clear spirit of clear fire" which rests upon the rigging does not reside within the human heart. Modern psychology knows it. The Bible knows it. "The heart is deceitful above all things," says Jeremiah, "and desperately wicked. Who can know it?" Even Ahab knew this when he searched his heart with such light as the darkened humanities still provided. But Ahab could not be humbled, like Job, nor rendered obedient, like Jonah. The case of Jonah, the subject of Father Mapple's sermon, should be recalled at this point—why else is that sermon there? Jonah's sin, the Father said, "was in his wilful disobedience of the command of God. . . . And if we obey God, we must disobey ourselves; and it is in this disobeying ourselves, wherein the hardness of obeying God consists." The submission of our own will to God is hard because it is, as Blake said of forgiveness, "a little death in the divine image," and this is a death that Ahab will not and cannot die. The corposants are saying, in effect:

Wilt thou even disannul my judgment?
Wilt thou condemn me that thou mayst be justified?

Job's answer the world knows; but Ahab, like his spiritual ancestor King Ahab, when confronted with Elijah, hardened his heart from turning to the Lord. A Hasidic maxim says: "There is no room for God in him who is full of himself." So full of himself is Ahab that, as a supreme act of folly, he grasps the harpoon, lately baptized in the devil's name but now tipped with a "flame of pale, forked fire," the very form of flame that the Persians thought "the holiest on the altar," and brandishes it over the panic-stricken and half-mutinous crew. And then, since the force of example is greater than intimidation, he shows his own fearlessness by extinguishing the light. This act confirms the breaking of the quadrant. And so the storm which followed that first defiance of the heavenly light, but which had been interrupted for a moment by God's warning finger, now bursts into renewed fury. It is a counterpart of the renewed fury which now rages in Ahab's mind, a fury so great that many of the mariners ran from him "in a terror of dismay."

The account of the external storm progresses from nightwatch to midnight, and from place to place, in close correspondence with the description of the storm which followed upon the oath of vengeance. The correspondence can hardly be accidental, for this second storm is but a logical fulfilment of the first, just as the look of triumph on the Parsee's face is a logical fulfilment of the low laugh that echoed from the hold.

The wonderful speech in which Ahab defies the corposants must not be passed over lightly; for it is just there that his tragic stature reaches its full height. He acknowledges the character of that light—it is the divine creative fire; it is his "fiery father" and, by implication, the father of all living things. It is the God whom once "as Persian" he did worship. But experience has taught him this: "To neither love nor reverence wilt thou be kind; and e'en for hate thou canst but kill; and all are killed." Whatever it is that Ahab means by "love," whether the love of God or the love of wife and child or the love of created things, it is an emotion difficult to verify. Reverence he may have felt toward that heavenly light—the reverence of a self-respecting servant toward a righteous master. But the supposedly righteous master has turned out to be a double-dealer, and so: "I now know thee, thou clear spirit, and I now know that thy right worship is defiance."

While Ahab thus defies the "lofty, tri-pointed trinity of flames," standing erect "with fixed upward eye and high-flung right arm," his foot is upon the kneeling Parsee. And this is right; for the Parsee knows his God, as Mephistopheles and Satan do, although his function is, like theirs, to seduce men from that knowledge.

The defiance in this scene is not without nobility. The corposants, as Ahab sees them, are deity indeed, but only the deity's power and glory; they know not pity and compassion. They are abstract power, impersonal, careless of the "personality," the unique Ahab, who confronts them. Yet love and pity and compassion, the affirmation of the unique and irreplaceable personality, must be somewhere—in some cosmic mother, could she but be found. As for the cosmic father, whose child he is, father and son are both fire, and their relationship is one of hate, not love, the child returning fire for fire. It is a part of Ahab's tragedy that he sees no difference in these two fires. The clear white fire that rests upon the rigging is fire transmuted into light; the passion in Ahab's breast is light regressed to fire.

The fires mount to thrice their previous height, and Ahab's spirit mounts to meet them. So blinding is the light that he closes his eyes and covers them with his right hand, while with his left he still holds the links. The lightning flashes through his skull, his eyeballs ache, his brain is stunned. No matter: "Yet blindfold, yet will I talk to thee. Light though thou be, thou leapest out of darkness; but I am darkness leaping out of light, leaping out of thee!" There is the formulation of a thought which for some time has been laboring toward birth in Ahab's mind, born now of the quickening power of light. In this thought there is more than defiance, there is a kind of triumph. But can such words be uttered? What will the pitiless power do? Blind him? The current slackens, he opens his eyes. Yes, he can see. "There burn the flames!" There is pity somewhere, a compassionate feminine, as a counterpart to the cruel masculine. "Oh, thou magnanimous! now I do glory in my genealogy. But thou art but my fiery father: my sweet mother, I know not. Oh, cruel! what hast thou done with her?"

This train of thought was first enunciated in the speech occasioned by the dying whale, wherein Ahab addressed, almost prayerfully, an infidel queen, a queen of death. And now, in his first speech to the corpusants, it is by virtue of a "queenly personality" that Ahab defies his "fiery father." "I own thy speechless, placeless power . . . yet while I earthly live, the queenly personality lives in me, and feels her royal rights." Immediately comes an unexpected breakdown in morale, a pathetic admission of the need for love and pity and compassion in place of hate. "But war is pain, and hate is woe. Come in thy lowest form of love, and I will kneel and kiss thee; but at thy highest, . . . there's that in here that still remains indifferent."

In all this Ahab was speaking as a pagan, even as a weary pagan might have spoken two thousand years ago. All along the shores of the Mediterranean the weary pagan world turned longingly to the Great Mother, she of many names and one reward, the reward of peace. When Ahab was in college, fixing his fiery lance (as Captain Peleg said) in the wonders of man's mind, he would surely have lowered for Plutarch and Apuleius. In Apuleius—to take him alone—Lucius prays to the queen of heaven, whether she be Ceres, Venus, Proserpine, or still another:

"By whatsoever name or fashion or shape it is lawful to call upon Thee, I pray Thee to end my great travail and misery and raise up my fallen hopes, and deliver me from the wretched fortune which so long time pursued me."

The goddess heard his prayer, and appeared before him in a dream, saying:

"I am she that is the natural mother of all things, mistress and governess of all the elements, the initial progeny of worlds, chief of the powers divine, queen of all that are in hell, the principal of them that dwell in heaven, manifested alone and under one form of all the gods and goddesses. At my will the planets of the sky, the wholesome winds of the seas, and the lamentable silences of hell be disposed; my name, my divinity, is adored throughout all the world, in divers manners, in variable customs, and by many names."

By whatever name she was worshiped, she was a nature-goddess, and she was sometimes represented as being prior to the Creator. One of her names was Isis, another Ishtar. As Ishtar, she was the female consort of Baal, the alien nature-god to whom King Ahab set up an altar and whom he served and worshiped. The analogy is, I suppose, fortuitous. Ahab turns to the mother as mankind has always done when the need for love and compassion becomes imperative. The medieval, as well as the ancient, world sought consolation in the mother; and in far-off China where, in Taoist theory, the world is seen as the interplay of two principles, a masculine and a feminine, the dark feminine principle is born at the very moment when the masculine becomes dominant. But Ahab turns to the mother in a definitely pagan way. His question, "O cruel, what hast thou done with her?" was a Gnostic question. Whether it is that in his emotional crisis he discovers ancient modes of thought or whether it is something else, his thinking, as he approaches and lives through the great crisis of his life is pagan thinking.

He carries his cosmology still further. The feminine principle, the "sweet mother," is the eternal night from whom the light itself and all created things have sprung. The mother is therefore primordial and eternal, the father temporal and derivative. The idea of Night as the primordial mother is as old as Hesiod and as new as Faust. In Hesiod's *Theogony* it is said: "Verily at first Chaos came to be. . . . From Chaos came forth Erebus and black Night, but of Night were born Aether and Day, whom she conceived and bare from union in love with Erebus." In *Faust* Mephistopheles includes the idea of usurpation (by no means for the first time):

> Part of that Part am I, once All, in primal Night,
> Part of the Darkness which brought forth the Light,
> The haughty Light, which now disputes the space,
> And claims of Mother Night her ancient place.

Knowing all this, Ahab knows a secret concerning the heavenly tyrant. On the doorstep of eternity the cruel father is but a foundling. A similar secret gives Prometheus patience and fortitude:

To me Zeus counts as less than nothing.
Let him work his will, show forth his power
for his brief day, his little moment
of lording it in heaven.

But Prometheus' motive lies in pity, Ahab's in pride. Pity can endure; pride, if wounded, seeks revenge. The father does, indeed, have his "incommunicable riddle" and his "unparticipated grief," like Ahab. He also has his pride. In his ignorance of his true beginning, he calls himself unbegun. But Ahab's "scorched eyes do dimly see" a truth hidden from the father. He can therefore say: "I know that of me, which thou knowest not of thyself, oh, thou omnipotent." What Ahab knows is what he dared to say at the beginning, an utterance for which he half expected to be blinded: "Light though thou be, thou leapest out of darkness; but I am darkness leaping out of light, leaping out of thee!" His uneasy conscience is justified at last. In the name of the dark mother he hurls defiance at the flaming father. Yet the mother is but a name; her existence is a theory, not an experience. He needs and wants the love she symbolizes, but, having no love with which to seek, he cannot find. What he can and does find is a bit of filial sympathy with the father, who also must have his mystery and grief. He, too, it is implied, may be a rebel. Something they have in common; they can burn together. "Leap! leap up, and lick the sky! I leap with thee; I burn with thee; would fain be welded with thee; defyingly I worship thee!" Defiance is true worship. It is true worship to will to be one's self.

It is in this grand and tragic speech, which must be read entire to be appreciated, that the intellectual aspect of Ahab's pursuit of Moby Dick reaches its climax. In part, it is a pursuit of the eternal mystery—a mystery as elusive as Moby Dick, a mystery, in fact, embodied in Moby Dick; and it is this that makes of Ahab a tragic figure and gives a metaphysical quality to his story. It is this that justifies us in seeing intellect in the deepening furrows upon his brow, in his crushing peddler's pack, in his sense that the burden of all the generations since Adam rests upon his shoulders. And yet, as he reaches the height of his nobility, he reaches the height of his self-delusion. He justifies defiance in the name of a mother not found but only sought, not sought in purity of heart but in double-mindedness, and hence not found. The fallacious union with the fiery father is, in the end, more real. He may think, for the moment, that he has solved his problem, but the answer that he has found is wrong. What he needed was a principle of self-control; what he found was a justification of the principle he had. The wrong answer, masquerading as a solution, cannot heal the inner strife; it can only feed and free the restive demon. Never is Ahab so demonic as in this moment of rational delusion. He grasps the harpoon lately tempered in heathen blood and blows out the sacred fire that tipped it. He brandishes it wildly above his head. The sailors flee as from a hurricane.

This hurricane, or rather the natural one which follows it, we have met before; in fact, we have lived through it. Next morning the wind blows strong and fair; the sky is light, but the sun, at the moment, is still invisible; the sea is "as a crucible of molten gold." The day before, it will be remembered, Ahab swore to guide his course by level reckoning—the level ship's compass, and the level dead reckoning of log and line. A curse upon all things that lift man's eyes to heaven. Man is to be the measure of all things. Ahab is to be the measure of all things. Now comes the test of this new measurement.

Ahab observes the sun's rays fore and aft, and especially the blending of the yellow rays with his "undeviating wake":

> "Ha, ha, my ship! thou mightest well be taken now for the sea-chariot of the sun. Ho, ho! all ye nations before my prow, I bring the sun to ye! Yoke on the further billows; hallo! a tandem, I drive the sea!"

It is obvious that Ahab's newly declared defiance has only deepened the neurosis. His new understanding of good and evil has only made him capable of believing, under the appropriate emotional stimulation, that he has become as God. But some protesting bit of sanity demands that the compasses be consulted. He consults them—"and lo! the two compasses pointed East, and the Pequod was as infallibly going West." For a moment Ahab almost seemed to stagger. The white light from heaven couldn't shake him, but the supposition that he might be mistaken could. Furthermore, the homeward direction of the "Pequod" and the fair wind following could be understood by a sensitive mind like Starbuck's, and even by the insensitive mind of the crew, as an omen at the least, if not as God's finger laid once again upon that ship. A natural explanation must be found. Ahab is not long in finding one. "I have it! It has happened before. Mr. Starbuck, last night's thunder turned our compasses—that's all."

Defiance continues, in both words and deeds. Words

first: "But Ahab is lord over the level loadstone yet."
Then deeds. He finds a piece of steel, fashions it to its
new function, works over it like a true craftsman, adds
some hocus-pocus to magnetize it, or to magnetize the
crew, and lo! "Look ye, for yourselves, if Ahab be not
lord of the level loadstone! The sun is East, and that
compass swears it!" The sailors looked, one after
another, and found it, to their amazement, even so.
Starbuck couldn't bear to watch the performance. He
looked away. Ishmael looked and saw its significance:
"In his fiery eyes of scorn and triumph, you then saw
Ahab in all his fatal pride."

A few hours later, the second means of level reckoning was tried—the log and line. The log was heaved, but
the line broke. "But Ahab can mend all." Rather, he
can give the necessary orders. Let the carpenter make
another log; let the old Manxman mend the line. But
the old Manxman, wise with the wisdom of many years,
is troubled. "There he goes now; to him nothing's happened; but to me, the skewer seems loosening out of the
middle of the world."

But defiance is not the whole of Ahab. Even at the
top of his bent, while he was flinging defiance at the
corposants, the need for love broke through. "But war
is pain and hate is woe. Come in thy lowest form of
love, and I will kneel and kiss thee; but at thy highest,
come as mere supernal power"—to that he will not
yield.

Well, there at his feet lies Pip, a counterpart of Ahab
in loneliness and sorrow, yes, in madness, both being
daft, as the Manxman says, one with strength and one
with weakness. It is appropriate that the power and the

glory, stooping to take the form of love in answer to Ahab's prayer, should choose Pip as a theophany. For madness, as people used to think, is touched with sanctity; and hence it is that Ahab cries out in protest to the Manxman: "Hands off from that holiness!" There was a special reason in Pip's case for thinking of him as sacred. As he lay on the cruel bosom of the sea, abandoned and alone, a chink opened in his finite armor and the infinite flowed in. "He saw God's foot upon the treadle of the loom, and spoke it." There, then, is the form of love which Ahab solemnly promised to worship if it should come—Pip the castaway, pleading for love to strengthen his own weakness and offering love, in turn, to Ahab to be an element of human weakness in his inhuman strength. For the first time in the story, for the first time in his life perhaps, compassion springs up in Ahab's breast. "Oh God! that man should be a thing for immortal souls to sieve through!" A pagan sentiment, and specifically a Hermetic sentiment. But the compassion that Ahab feels for Pip is not now or ever pure and simple. It is always checked and crossed by some form of self-affirmation—at the moment by accusation of the gods:

"There can be no hearts above the snow-line. Oh, ye frozen heavens! look down here. Ye did beget this luckless child, and have abandoned him, ye creative libertines. Here, boy; Ahab's cabin shall be Pip's home henceforth, while Ahab lives. Thou touchest my inmost centre, boy; thou art tied to me by cords woven of my heart-strings. Come, let's down."

"What's this? here's velvet shark-skin," intently gazing at Ahab's hand, and feeling it. "Ah, now, had poor Pip but felt so kind a thing as this, perhaps he had ne'er been lost! This seems to me, sir, as a man-rope; something that weak souls may hold by. Oh, sir, let old Perth now come and rivet these two hands together; the black one with the white, for I will not let this go."

The scene recalls the taking of the Oath, where hands were spliced in a far different fellowship. Further afield it recalls Coriolanus' son beseeching his proud father to be compassionate:

> This boy, that cannot tell what he would have,
> But kneels and holds up hands for fellowship.

Together they go down into the cabin. "Come!" says Ahab, "I feel prouder leading thee by thy black hand, than though I grasped an Emperor's!" So far, the call for love has but heightened pride. The humility which alone could save has not awakened. The old Manxman's comment, ending the chapter, is a subtle one:

"But here's the end of the rotten line—all dripping, too. Mend it, eh? I think we had best have a new line altogether. I'll see Mr. Stubb about it."

As time passes, a struggle takes place below, unreported but surely comparable with that other unreported struggle which Ahab underwent prior to his appearance on the quarter-deck. It would seem that a relationship hitherto unknown to Ahab had sprung up, a new line of thinking, a life of dialogue not command, the relationship of I and Thou, Thou being another I. A life of love in the cabin begins to challenge a life of hate on deck. It is a crisis; and Ahab, always sane enough to know that he is mad and mad enough to be in love with madness, faces the issue clearly and makes the expected mad decision:

"There is that in thee, poor lad, which I feel too curing to my malady. Like cures like; and for this hunt, my malady becomes my most desired health."

He plays, double-mindedly, with the idea of Pip being captain, captain in Ahab's chair below, while Ahab is in command on deck. But the single-minded love of Pip sees this delusion:

> "No, no, no! ye have not a whole body, sir; do ye but use poor me for your one lost leg; only tread upon me, sir; I ask no more, so I remain a part of ye. . . .
> "They tell me, sir, that Stubb did once desert poor little Pip, whose drowned bones now show white, for all the blackness of his living skin. But I will never desert ye, sir, as Stubb did him. Sir, I must go with ye."
> "If thou speakest thus to me much more, Ahab's purpose keels up in him. I tell thee no; it cannot be."
> "Oh good master, master, master!"
> "Weep so, and I will murder thee! have a care, for Ahab too is mad."

This is the form of love that Ahab had called for, and now that it has come, he threatens it with murder. Here is a problem in psychology that requires me once again to resort to Kierkegaard. But, since the problem is related to the demonic character and the concept of dread, one may look with confidence to that source for light.

One fact, then, that Keirkegaard notes about the demonic person is that he lives in dread of the good. The good would integrate his divided psyche, it would heal the neurosis. But, in so doing, it would make of Ahab a different person, one that he fears to become. True, he dreads to remain the man he is, having found that war is pain and hate is woe. But he dreads still more the responsibilities of peace and freedom. He is like a nation that wants peace, but not at the price of its sovereign identity. As Kierkegaard points out, rather needlessly for the contemporary reader, the demonic personality has two wills, a weaker one demanding release, a stronger one demanding imprisonment. If Ahab begged for love, it was more in anger than in sorrow. He belongs to that class of neurotics who do not really wish to be cured.

More subtly, Kierkegaard points out that there is a kind and degree of compassion which is only a protection to one's own egoism:

> Only when the compassionate person is so related by his compassion to the sufferer that in the strictest sense he comprehends that it is his own cause which is here in question, only when he knows how to identify himself in such a way with the sufferer that when he is fighting for an explanation he is fighting for himself, renouncing all thoughtlessness, softness, and cowardice, only then does compassion acquire significance, and only then does it perhaps find a meaning.

Some of Ahab's compassion is of the protective, egotistical sort; but some of it threatens to break through and create a new center of consciousness. There is danger of a struggle to the death between Pip and Ahab. Hubert, in *King John*, is faced with the same dilemma, in the presence of young Arthur:

> If I talk to him, with his innocent prate
> He will awake my mercy, which lies dead.

Hubert weakens; but Ahab, mad by his own confession, remains strong. "Come in thy lowest form of love," and I will worship thee, Ahab had promised; but it was a promise that he could not keep. A half-hearted promise to worship eventuated in a wholehearted threat to kill.

More subtly still, Kierkegaard observes that he who lives in dread lives in dread of guilt and fate. Of guilt it might be said, at first thought, that it is a conception which never enters into Ahab's consciousness. It dare not, for it would entail repentance and, on the heels of that, the liberation which he also dreads. It would involve him, if accepted, in the whole world's guilt and would demand that he bear the burden, not only in justice, but redemptively. But guilt is not a feeling easily disposed of. It may be feared, but, as Kierkegaard points out, it exercises fascination as well as fear. This paradoxical relationship of the demonic personality to guilt seems to be exemplified in Ahab. He will presently admit the fact, though not the guilt, of a loveless life. But the guilt, as well as the fact, of blasphemy can hardly be evaded. But does Ahab look "almost desirously," as Kierkegaard says, at guilt? A decisive answer is impossible; but what, it may be asked, is the significance of those soul-satisfying talks with Pip? "Now, then, Pip," says Ahab, "we'll talk this over; I do suck most wondrous philosophies from thee!" What can this wondrous wisdom be except some inspired babble that makes Ahab's purpose keel up within him? Something that suggests that the mystery of pain can only be understood by embracing it? Something that suggests the guilt, and the folly, too, of willing in despair to be one's self?

And then there is the dread of fate. This dread is an ever present undercurrent in Ahab's mind, as inseparable from him as the ivory shaft of hate on which he walks. It is, in part, a sense of impending ill, a dread of the day to come. On the day before the last day of all, this anxiety suddenly broke out with reference to the evil omens. "The things called omens! And yesterday I talked the same to Starbuck there, concerning my broken boat. Oh! how valiantly I seek to drive out of others' hearts what's clinched so fast in mine!" And today, that fatal day of double-mindedness for Ahab, his heart is troubled about tomorrow, and what it may bring to Pip:

"Listen, and thou wilt often hear my ivory foot upon the deck, and still know that I am there. And now I quit thee. Thy hand!—Met! True art thou, lad, as the circumference to its centre. So: God for ever bless thee; and if it come to that,—God for ever save thee, let what will befall."

But Ahab is not true, as circumference to center, unless self be taken as the center. He needn't leave it to God to save Pip in this world; he could do it himself by a change of heart and a change of course. Somewhere there must have been another low laugh of triumph from the Parsee.

A few days ago, the corposants above deck; today, Pip below deck. Heaven has been twice defied. Power has warned, and love has pled, but the "Pequod" holds her course.

X

The "Pequod" holds her course, again, heedless of a sister-ship in need, its commander having no love for his neighbor, even though his neighbor was a whaling captain from Nantucket. It has been a long time since we have met a returning ship, but two are coming on now in quick succession.

The first is the "Rachel," looking the distress she feels. Obviously, she needs help; but Ahab, conscious only of his own need, breaks in with his own question: "Hast seen the White Whale?" Yes, only yesterday; and the captain has lost a son. Will Ahab join the search? Stubb would. Anyone would—anyone but Ahab. Captain

Gardiner pleads with Captain Ahab, as one parent to another, as one asking Ahab to do as he would be done by. But Ahab's emotional responses have been killed. He foresaw this consequence and accepted it when he assumed the iron crown; he enacts it now:

"Avast," cried Ahab—"touch not a rope-yarn"; then in a voice that prolongingly moulded every word—"Captain Gardiner, I will not do it. Even now I lose time. Good bye, good bye. God bless ye, man, and may I forgive myself, but I must go."

Captain Gardiner must go, too; in three minutes he must go; three minutes by the binnacle watch. And yet there is in this dismissal a minute misgiving, a trace of human kindness. Had Ahab said, "May God forgive me," I would have thought the expression merely rhetorical. But "May I forgive myself"—what a depth of revelation in that phrase! The problem of self-forgiveness is well known to the psychiatrist. Dr. Jung discusses it:

Perhaps this sounds very simple, but simple things are always the most difficult. In actual life it requires the greatest discipline to be simple, and the acceptance of oneself is the essence of the moral problem and the epitome of a whole outlook upon life. That I feed the hungry, that I forgive an insult, that I love my enemy in the name of Christ—all these are undoubtedly great virtues. What I do unto the least of my brethren, that I do unto Christ. But what if I should discover that the least among them all, the poorest of all the beggars, the most impudent of all the offenders, the very enemy himself—that these are within me, and that I myself stand in need of the alms of my own kindness—that I myself am the enemy who must be loved—what then?

Dr. Jung goes on to say that some persons escape from themselves by taking an interest in others; but some cannot do this and succumb to a neurosis. I have no doubt that a phase of Ahab's neurosis was the need to be forgiven. I have no doubt also that he never forgave himself. Forgiveness was simply outside his experience. The Christian solves his problem by believing in God's forgiveness and by forgiving others in his turn. But godless Ahab is imprisoned in his unforgiving ego. He dies unforgiving and unforgiven, except by a God whom he did not know.

After a suitable but short interval, there comes another ship—the last one—named the "Delight." It, too, has encountered Moby Dick; only yesterday it lost five men, four of them going down without the rites of burial. The captain is unnamed. Dare we think of him as Everyman, waging a losing battle with the world's evil? But the ship is named the "Delight," a name which is surely meant to recall the theme of Father Mapple's sermon. Certain it is, however, that the vessel is not reaching the end of its long journey in the triumphant spirit of Father Mapple. The white ribs of its shattered lifeboat suggest the bleaching skeleton of a horse. Is all this a melancholy commentary on the sermon, an instance of the shadow that falls between word and deed? "But oh! my shipmates!" cried the Father, "on the starboard hand of every woe there is a sure delight; and higher the top of that delight than the bottom of the woe is deep." Does the unnamed captain stick doggedly to this faith? We cannot tell for certain. There seems to be reverence as well as fear in his report of Moby Dick, and sincerity in his conduct of a Christian burial. Perhaps Everyman—if he is Everyman—is considered to come through with courage but with only a little faith. However that may be, the captain has an eye for the ironic. As the "Pequod" turned hurriedly away, the strange coffin-like buoy hanging at its stern came into conspicuous relief:

"Ha! yonder! look yonder, men!" cried a foreboding voice in her wake. "In vain, oh, ye strangers, ye fly our sad burial; ye but turn us your taffrail to show us your coffin!"

In these events and in the period of their occurrence, Ahab sinks to the nadir of his career. The whole crew seems to be caught up and congealed in his web of hate. If any wholesomeness remains, it lives in hiding. Fear and suspicion, as well as hate, take possession of Ahab's mind. There is scarcely anyone that he dares to trust. Even Stubb and Flask are secretly suspected. In Starbuck alone does he retain a certain restricted degree of faith. Is it faith in Starbuck's feebleness of will or in his rightness of mind? Ahab has had reason to have trust in both.

The Parsee returns after what seems like a considerable absence. His figure seems more strange and tenuous than ever, partly because his time is very near and partly because, as Ahab's counterpart, his mental light is burning very low. Tremulous and shadowy as he is, he is intense and tyrannous, like Ahab; so that "even as Ahab's eyes so awed the crew's, the inscrutable Parsee's glance awed his." Neither of them seemed to sleep, neither went below; day and night both kept unbroken watch. Hardly a word passed between them. What need of intercourse? The life of the mind had sunk to just one thing—the restless search for Moby Dick. Hate has frozen thought and the very capacity to think:

Here's food for thought, had Ahab time to think; but Ahab never thinks; he only feels, feels, feels; *that's* tingling enough for mortal man! to think's audacity. God only has that right and privilege. Thinking is, or ought to be, a coolness and a calmness; and our poor hearts throb, and our poor brains beat too much for that. And yet, I've sometimes thought my brain was very calm—frozen calm, this old skull cracks so, like a glass in which the contents turned to ice, and shiver it. And still this hair is growing now; this moment growing, and heat must breed it; but no, it's like that sort of common grass that will grow anywhere, between the earthy clefts of Greenland ice or in Vesuvius lava.

Nature, too, has her revenges and is taking them on her revengeful child. The emotional responses may be killed, but the killing won't stop there. The senses are the natural feeders of the mind; if they are frozen, with what shall the mind think?

In some of the great tragedies there is a moment of profound insight, so that the protagonist proceeds to his fate enlightened and in a sense content. There now comes a chapter entitled "The Symphony," which performs a similar function. The day is warm, the sky is clear. Masculine sea and feminine air meet and mingle in an all-pervading azure. The sundered contraries, whose union in man the microcosm, or in the universe the macrocosm, brings serenity and fulfilment, are enjoying that rare union now. Never before have the contraries been conjoined in Ahab, nor in the universe as he has apprehended it. The masculine contrary has revealed to his cruel gaze only its cruelty; while the feminine contrary has eluded him entirely—"Where art thou, my sweet mother?" But now the more cruel aspects of the masculine sea—the whales, swordfish, and sharks—are subdued and deep down below the surface, while the feminine air is cloven by the snow-white wings of birds, symbolizing its kindly thoughts. So enchanting was the scene, so affectionate the sky and air, that Ahab yielded to the sweet influences and dropped a tear. Now a tear, Blake says, "is an intellectual thing"; it is so in this instance. For somehow the benediction resting upon air and sea and sky has made a break-through, where the corposants and Pip could not. Into Ahab's mind, for once quiescent, wisdom has come at last to sit in judgment, and the judgment is, in one word, Folly. Ahab accepts the verdict but explains it away, as far as possible. The sea has done it—forty years of warfare on the pitiless sea, forty years of solitude and dry, unsalted fare, "fit emblem of the dry nourishment of my soul! . . . And then, the madness, the frenzy, the boiling blood and the smoking brow, with which, for a thousand lowerings old Ahab has furiously, foamingly chased his prey—more a demon than a man!—aye, aye! what a forty years' fool—fool—old fool, has old Ahab been!" The end of it all is a sense of intolerable age, a back breaking with its burden of hate, a joyless heart. The disillusioned old man turns, in his momentary wisdom, from the scrutiny of sea and sky and the abstractions of good and evil to an unfailing source of light, a kindly human eye, the eye of Starbuck, who stands beside him:

"Close! stand close to me, Starbuck; let me look into a human eye; it is better than to gaze into sea or sky; better than to gaze upon God. By the green land; by the bright hearth-stone! this is the magic glass, man; I see my wife and my child in thine eye. No, no; stay on board, on board!— lower not when I do; when branded Ahab gives chase to Moby Dick. That hazard shall not be thine. No, no! not with the far away home I see in that eye!"

The moment of illumination is but a moment, yet it is essential to the tragedy and to the conflict underlying it. This is the culmination of one element of the neurosis—the humanities. Previously, when they have tried to put their case, they have addressed a mind beclouded with passion and hardened with pride; but now, as by an act of grace, Ahab's mind is as calm and clear as his environment. Truth can speak out at last and be recognized as truth. But soon the defense speaks up. It is the Parsee's turn. Not present, as yet, in person but present in Ahab's mind, he speaks his piece. Let the hunt continue, he says, it is the easy way, it is Ahab's way, it is the Puritan, the Parsee way. As the Parsee's whispered words take increasing hold of Ahab's mind, the truth comes to seem far off and dreamlike. At the same time, Starbuck steals away unnoticed, and Ahab, crossing the deck to gaze over on the other side, finds the Parsee there beside him, leaning over the same rail. In Swedenborg's heaven the angels change their positions instantly in accordance with the state of their affections. So it is with Ahab. When, in the Parsee's absence, the humanities were for a moment uppermost, Starbuck came to his side unsummoned. When the inhumanities regained control, the Parsee, also unsummoned, was there beside him.

In dissociating himself from Starbuck and crossing the deck to join the Parsee, Ahab made his final choice. If it has been long delayed, it is because Ahab's spirit had to be tried many times and in many ways before it could make the tragic choice of evil, seeing and acknowledging the good. Hitherto the issue has not been tragically clear. In the struggle with Pip there was too much pride and passion for a clear and reasoned judgment. Today, however, the sky cleared in Ahab's mind, the light of reason shone, and right and wrong stood separate and distinct. But when Starbuck urged the adoption of the right and heading the ship around in the direction of Nantucket, Ahab refused.

> Knowledge we ask not—knowledge Thou hast lent,
> But, Lord, the will—there lies our bitter need.

In the hour of need Ahab failed. The light broke through into the darkness of his mind, and the darkness extinguished it. That very night, in the mid-watch, Ahab smelled a whale. In the morning, sight verified smell. "There she blows!—there she blows! A hump like a snow-hill! It is Moby Dick!"

The logic of Moby Dick's appearance at this moment is perfect. So long as some light of faith remained in Ahab's mind, Moby Dick remained elusive. Recently, when the light was burning very low, Moby Dick had been reported. And now, the wrong choice having been made calmly and deliberately, that monstrous apparition of evil turns up immediately, right under Ahab's nose. This eventuality became inevitable—almost—when Ahab broke the quadrant. As he said himself, some time thereafter, "So far gone am I in the dark side of earth, that its other side, the theoretic bright one, seems but uncertain twilight to me." During that twilight period, numerous signs and portents happened, bearing the appearance of providential intervention; but Ahab drove on, into the dark, defying augury. "By light, light," the ancient motto ran; and, conversely, one might say, "By night, night, and the terrors of the night."

This, whether recognized or not, is a law of life, and it is a law of Ahab's life, unrecognized. As we are, so do we see; and as we see, so are we. Let it be understood that doing is included, so that the law may be and has been stated thus: "If we see things as they are, we shall live as we ought; and if we live as we ought, we shall see things as they are." Man's history could be written in terms of what vision the human imagination has been able to reach and hold. Blake so wrote it; and once said sadly of Los, the agent of that vision—"He became what he beheld." What Ahab beheld was the specter of evil in the world. Daily and nightly it possessed him until evil became more real than good—the only reality, in fact. For selfish reasons, and yet not altogether selfishly, he was determined to stalk down the specter and be avenged. But hate and vengeance are evil means and not a medium to good ends, for the means, in practice, become the ends. So Ahab became himself a portion of the evil he beheld and fell a victim to the very specter he was seeking to destroy.

Could it have been otherwise? Is it possible to conceive of Ahab undergoing a mutation and rising, an integrated man, into a new life lived from a new center? Dostoevski might have managed it, but he would, I think, have had to fashion Ahab a little differently. For in Ahab's review of his entire life there is something lacking to conversion. There is the acknowledgment of defeat and the sentence of folly, but there is no sense of guilt, no evidence of a broken and a contrite heart. There is, indeed, along with the momentary pangs of regret, a certain subdued pride in the thousand landings and the mad pursuits. Certainly, there is in his far more pagan than Puritan heart no sense of sin. St. Augustine, as a young man and a Manichaean, wrestled with Ahab's problem and resisted conversion because, like Ahab, he was unwilling to find evil in himself. For a long time he anxiously sought "whence is evil?" and made the very mistake that Ahab made; he "sought in an evil way, and saw not the evil in [his] very search." Not soon did he discover that evil was "no substance, but a perversion of the will turned aside from Thee, O God." Slowly did he come to recognize certain truths in the New Testament which were not to be found in the books of the Platonists. "No man says there"—in the aforesaid books—"Shall not my soul be submitted unto God? . . . No man there hears Him call, Come unto Me, all ye that labour." But the seeds of conversion were in him all the time—in the fact, for instance, that he "trembled exceedingly," that he "trembled with love and awe." But in Ahab there was no love, no awe, no trembling, no desire to be submitted unto God. Yet resignation of the old life is a necessary prelude to a new one. In Kierkegaard's analysis, resignation—infinite resignation—is the stage just prior to faith. The penitent makes infinite resignation and then regains everything in a different mode and as a different man. But the infinite resignation "is that shirt we read about in the old fable. The thread is spun under tears, the cloth bleached with tears, the shirt sewn with tears; but then too it is a better protection than iron and steel." Ahab's single tear would not have woven a man-sized shirt; and its source was not in resignation, but rather in a resigned despair "that wills to be itself, to be itself in terms of its misery." If Plato is right, Ahab possessed "the power of learning the truth and the organ to see it with," but, "just as one might have to turn the whole body round in order that the eye should see light instead of darkness, so the entire soul" would have to turn around in order to enter into a new life. But this was a conversion that Ahab, being Ahab, could not or would not make. Had he made it, he would have turned the "Pequod" around. Despairingly, he willed to be his miserable self and to push on into the dark.

Did Ahab will it, or another? Ahab thought: someone or something else:

"What is it, what nameless, inscrutable, unearthly thing is it; what cozening, hidden lord and master, and cruel, remorseless emperor commands me; that against all natural lovings and longings, I so keep pushing, and crowding, and jamming myself on all the time; recklessly making me ready to do what in my own proper, natural heart, I durst not so much as dare? Is Ahab, Ahab? Is it I, God, or who, that lifts this arm?"

It is necessity. Sun and moon, he goes on to say, are servants of natural law, and how can man be less?

"By heaven, man, we are turned round and round in this world, like yonder windlass, and Fate is the handspike. And all the time, lo! that smiling sky, and this unsounded sea!"

Necessity in sun and stars, freedom in sky and sea. The antinomy has vexed the world. On the human level it has been expressed by the dualism of the natural man, in a state of bondage to the natural world, and the spiritual man, who may transcend it. Is this transcendence a free and open choice? Ahab thinks not. Faith thinks that it is, whether Christian faith or Hindu faith or atheistic existential faith. When the decisive moment

comes, the latter says, in all its factuality, there is freedom with which to meet and deal with it—or not. De-
terminism, it says further, is but the "behavior of ex-
cuse." Of this view Ahab's conduct at this decisive
moment would be a prime example. Ahab sees the pre-
dicament of the natural man in the figure of a wheel.
The *Bhagavad Gita* uses the same figure in a kindlier
sense. "The Lord lives in the heart of every creature.
He turns them round and round upon the wheel of his
Maya." This is interpreted by S. Radhakrishnan as
meaning that the power that rules the world is not
careless of man's fate. On the contrary, it resides, with
beneficent intent, in every human heart. The Lord of
life is there, whether we choose to acknowledge him
or not. If we do acknowledge and obey him, "we will
resign all actions to God and escape from our ego."
But if we hug our ego and remain imprisoned, we must
be thrown back into existence again and yet again until
at last, freely and without constraint, we make full
surrender and attain full liberation. According to this
doctrine, Ahab must turn upon the wheel until he learns
that Fate is not its handspike.

But Fate has still another meaning, and Ahab, being
anxious to find a way to escape responsibility, makes
use of it. The Calvinist in him has recourse to the
theory of predestination. Talking with Starbuck, a
little later, he says:

"Starbuck, of late I've felt strangely moved to thee; ever
since that hour we both saw—thou know'st what, in one
another's eyes. But in this matter of the whale, be the front
of thy face to me as the palm of this hand—a lipless, un-
featured blank. Ahab is forever Ahab, man. This whole
act's immutably decreed. 'Twas rehearsed by thee and me
a billion years before this ocean rolled."

It must have been with profound relief that Ahab finally resigned his problem to the original author of his being, in the belief that his fate had been laid down before all worlds. This supposition explained him to himself and explained certain things away. First of all, there was the birthmark, the sign and seal of Fate, and then the prophecy, both borne out by the uncontrollable fits of passion, by the mysterious demonic drive that compelled him to belie his better self, by the sense that "some one thrusts these cards into these old hands of mine, [and] swears that I must play them and no others." It is such thoughts as these, arising in Ahab's mind, that take him across the deck to join the Parsee.

So Ahab is to remain forever Ahab. If there is in this self-affirmation an unconscious despair, there is also a conscious pride. "Proud as Greek god," Ahab once said of himself, and proudly he accepts his fate, knowing it to be his doom. No one could wish the conclusion to be other than it is. The aesthetic validity is so overpowering that other validities are hypothetical and irrelevant. "Samson hath quit himself like Samson." This sense of consistency has been the consolation of many a self-willed man looking back with some misgiving over the course of a long life. The play is almost over, let it proceed to its logical conclusion. Likewise, a young man, high-spirited and proud, may take pleasure in affirming the lifelong preservation of his identity. The youthful Donne loved the Spanish motto: "Rather dead than changed." Even the common man likes to see character stick. So Stubb, having overheard Ahab talking to himself about the cards being thrust into his hands, with orders to play them, commented:

"And damn me, Ahab, but thou actest right; live in the game, and die it!"

"There she blows!" It's Moby Dick! The boats are lowered, the Parsee standing, as usual, in Ahab's. "A pale, death-glimmer lit up Fedallah's sunken eyes; a hideous motion gnawed his mouth." But he soon regains his oriental calm; it is for the tiger-yellow crew—the savage harpooners—to provide the passion and the energy. He observes the chase and its vicissitudes with the indifference of one who, from the beginning, has known the end and accepts his fate. Suddenly he's missed. He has been tangled in the lines and dragged below. As he well knew, he was Ahab's pilot and fated to go first.

"There she blows!" How different she is from the cruel figment of Ahab's imagination. The sea is tranquil and spread out like a noon meadow, an exceeding rapture brooding over it, and in the midst a form so glorious that it suggested the white bull that Jupiter once became—a dazzling hump invested with a "gentle joyousness":

Before it, far out on the soft Turkish-rugged waters, went the glistening white shadow from his broad, milky forehead, a musical rippling playfully accompanying the shade; and behind, the blue waters interchangeably flowed over into the moving valley of his steady wake; and on either hand bright bubbles arose and danced by his side.

Is it not reasonable to see a symbolical quality in that description? It has a close analogy in the Job pictures of William Blake, where the monster of the sea (Leviathan) and the monster of the land (Behemoth) are invested, like Moby Dick, with joyousness. This insight, so dim to mortal sense, was revealed to Job, who is depicted as seeing, for the moment, as God sees. But Ahab's eyes were blinded by his obsession. Yet not completely. On the last day, with Moby Dick in sight, his mind is haunted by the vision of eternal beauty and its intimations of other goals than his:

"But let me have one more good round look aloft here at the sea; there's time for that. An old, old sight, and yet somehow so young; aye, and not changed a wink since I first saw it, a boy, from the sandhills of Nantucket! The same!— the same! the same to Noah as to me. There's a soft shower to leeward. Such lovely leewardings! They must lead some-where—to something else than common land, more palmy than the palms. Leeward! the white whale goes that way...."

The good moment is ended; and, tarrying just long enough to say goodbye to the old masthead, Ahab lowers for the last time. "For the third time my soul's ship starts upon this voyage, Starbuck." But the "Pequod" has been his soul's ship ever since the oath was taken.

Of course, that dazzling white embodies terror as well as beauty and serenity. Therein lies the mystery of good and evil. When aroused, Moby Dick can stave the lowered boats to splinters. Maddened, he can drive the solid white buttress of his forehead against the "Pequod" 's bow and sink it. But he would be willing to call it quits and avoid that final catastrophe. Star-buck, observing that Moby Dick is swimming rapidly away, begs Ahab to give up:

"Oh! Ahab," cried Starbuck, "not too late is it, even now, the third day, to desist. See! Moby Dick seeks thee not. It is thou, thou, that madly seekest him!"

But Ahab is no longer free to choose. Pride and pas-sion have delivered him into total darkness and total slavery. Of the total slavery the lack of any answer to Starbuck's plea may be taken as an indication; the total darkness is revealed in a helpless cry which, in its irony, becomes supremely tragic:

Ahab staggered; his hand smote his forehead. "I grow blind; hands! stretch out before me that I may yet grope my way. Is't night?"

He recovers sight, of a kind, but only to see the whale make for the "Pequod," whose crew stands enchanted and motionless before the white oncoming terror as it had stood motionless and enchanted before the white light of the corposants.

The ruling passion is strong in Ahab's death. Pride and pride-engendered hate. Pride in his gallant ship, pride or a proud despair in a lonely death ending a lonely life, pride in the consciousness that his "topmost greatness" lay in his "topmost grief." Hate in the final thrust: "From hell's heart I stab at thee; for hate's sake I spit my last breath at thee. Sink all coffins and all hearses to one common pool! and since neither can be mine, let me then tow to pieces, while still chasing thee, though tied to thee, thou damned whale! *Thus*, I give up the spear!"

Again—how often—yet once again, nature and the soul of man are linked together beyond all utterance. The fact that Ahab should be towed to pieces, tied, while still chasing it, to the damned whale!

Another such symbol is Ahab's dying gesture. "I turn my body from the sun. . . . Towards thee I roll, thou all-destroying but unconquering whale." The reader will remember that not so long ago a dying whale sank before Ahab's eyes, and, sinking, it turned its head toward the sun. A dim instinct, it would seem, told it where allegiance lay. "He too worships fire"; mused Ahab, "most faithful, broad, baronial vassal of the sun! . . . here, too, life dies sunwards full of faith." But faithless Ahab turns toward the whale—toward that symbol of all evil which has made an evil thing of him. But note that word "unconquering." Is it Ahab's final defiance of the enemy to whom he yields his body but not his spirit? Or is it another good moment, such as came to him at the sight of the "lovely leewardings"? Can it be that in the darkness of his mind a spark of light remained—a shred of faith which told him that Moby Dick, also, would have to yield some day, as he is yielding now? In that case there really would be, as Blake says, a limit to contraction.

If Ahab's last words boil up from the hell within, the author's final comment comes down from heaven above. For he so contrives it that a sky-hawk, having left "its natural home among the stars," is impaled on the "Pequod"'s mast and pulled down with Ahab's ship, "which, like Satan, would not sink to hell till she had dragged a living part of heaven along with her." At the same time, the bird provides the plumes for the hearse, even as the Parsee had foretold. Once again the imagery is inspired. For what the story says from the beginning is that nothing is wholly good or wholly evil. The attempt to separate the moral contraries and draw a line between them is dangerous, at best, and fatal if faith is dying down and self-righteousness is springing up. 'Tis better to let them remain obscured in the all-embracing and awe-inspiring coverage of white.

XI

The "Pequod" sank, and Ishmael alone escaped to tell the tale. Someone had to tell it, someone had to be saved. Therein lay a necessity which might have been met by some crude device, utterly at odds with the spirit of the story. Instead, it became a minor triumph. The person elected to be saved was Ishmael, the observer and narrator. The means of escape was a life-buoy, originally a canoe intended to serve as Queequeg's coffin. Queequeg, a South Sea islander and a headhunter, was yet simple, honest, and sincere, almost a noble savage, as the phrase used to be; a very different savage, certainly, from his companion savages and harpooners, Tashtego and Daggoo, and different especially in this, that he had religious faith. The story begins with a ritual of worship before his little god Yojo; and he kept his day-and-night-long fast—his Ramadan—with an absorption from the world that nothing could disturb. Now it happened that in the course of the voyage Queequeg came down with chills and fever. He wasted away to the thinness of a skeleton; only his eyes grew round and full and luminous; they seemed to be full of immortal longings. In the minds of all the crew, and in his own mind, as he lay in his hammock, rocking gently over the rolling waves, the end was near. But how should he enter decorously into the new life, the ethereal paradise, which his own faith and the faith of his race promised him? To be tossed into the sea as food for sharks—not that way, certainly; but rather, as it finally occurred to him, in a way "not unlike the custom of his own race, who, after embalming a dead warrior, stretched him out in his canoe, and so left him to be floated away to the starry archipelagoes; for not only do they believe that the stars are isles, but that far beyond all visible horizons, their own mild, uncontinented seas, interflow with the blue heavens; and so form the white breakers of the milky way." He therefore ordered a little Nantucket canoe to be made and provided with the pious requisites of such a voyage. But then he suddenly grew better and decided to postpone his death. Postpone it he could and would, he said; there was some little thing to be done ashore. Fate must have smiled, noting that his name was entered with the rest of the "Pequod" 's crew, for no distant time and place. And then it happened, before long, that the "Pequod" lost her life-buoy, and Queequeg hinted mysteriously that his coffin—his canoe—might take its place; and so it did. Queequeg had said to Ishmael, at the beginning of their friendship, that he would gladly die for him, if need should be. He did just that. For he went down with all the rest except Ishmael, who was floated away to safety on that strange life-buoy.

In those latitudes a day in the open sea is full of danger. What the waters spare the sharks may take. Ahab in his lowered boat was a special target for the sharks. "Whether it was that Ahab's crew were all such tiger yellow barbarians, and therefore their flesh more musky to the senses of the sharks—a matter sometimes well known to affect them—however it was, they seemed to follow that one boat without molesting the others."

And still as Ahab glided over the waves the unpitying sharks accompanied him; and so pertinaciously stuck to the boat; and so continually bit at the plying oars, that the blades became jagged and crunched, and left small splinters in the sea, at almost every dip.

"Heed them not! those teeth but give new rowlocks to your oars. Pull on! 'tis the better rest, the shark's jaw than the yielding water."

"But at every bite, sir, the thin blades grow smaller and smaller!"

"They will last long enough! pull on!—But who can tell"—he muttered—"whether these sharks swim to feast on the whale or on Ahab?"

Were the sharks attracted by a musky smell, or was it, symbolically, the attraction of like to like? However it may have been, it is a striking contrast that Ishmael's life-buoy was not molested. "The unharming sharks, they glided by as if with padlocks on their mouths; the savage sea-hawks sailed with sheathed beaks." Is it not reasonable to suppose that a spiritual principle was again at work, which rendered those cruel creatures impotent? Setting aside, or rather postponing, the character of Ishmael, can we not say that the coffin life-buoy itself was a sacred object, sacred enough to render the occupant inviolate? For it had been prepared by Queequeg in full faith, both as a coffin and as a life-buoy, a life-buoy in the sense that it was intended to convey his spirit to the life eternal. In the end, since Queequeg proved recalcitrant, it served Ishmael's need. The question then arises, Why was Ishmael chosen, rather than another?

The answer might come quickly: the narrator had to be saved; but this answer must go as quickly as it came. Another answer would be: The man to be saved should be a man of a little faith, could such a one be found, especially since it was lack of faith that ruined Ahab.

What, then, of Starbuck? He had moral instincts and

moral insight. He alone is reluctant to take the oath, and when, having given in, his stubbornness flares up again, the low, triumphant laugh of the Parsee, still hidden in the hold, dies away. From the first Starbuck knows that Ahab is mad; he once considers murder in order to avert the fate which he foresees for all the crew; he pleads with Ahab to return. It is in the light of Starbuck's eyes that Ahab reads the story of his life aright. As a harpooner he wields "the best lance out of all Nantucket," but his spiritual lance is frail. His evasion of the issue stirs Ishmael both to indignation and compassion. Indignation says that Starbuck, in an emergency, was a man of "mere unaided virtue." Compassion says that something deep within us "bleeds with keenest anguish at the undraped spectacle of a valor-ruined man." In the indignant report, what is the meaning of the phrase "mere unaided virtue"? Does it not mean: unaided by a power, not himself, that would have made for righteousness had Starbuck called it to his aid by faith? The very moment he capitulated, he murmured: "God keep me!—keep us all!" And a little later, at dusk, reflecting over the demonic element in Ahab's action, he exclaimed:

> "Oh, life! 'tis now that I do feel the latent horror in thee! but 'tis not in me! that horror's out of me, and with the soft feeling of the human in me, yet will I try to fight ye, ye grim, phantom futures! Stand by me, hold me, bind me, O ye blessed influences!"

True it is that the horror's not in Starbuck; true also that his determination to fight it weakens to the point of failure. He hasn't the strength of mind to comprehend Ahab's problem (as Ishmael has) nor the strength of will to do what he knows, instinctively, is right. Those sentiments are not expressions of the faith that saves, when the latent horror's out.

Starbuck's tragedy—and it is thought of as nothing less—stands out more clearly when polarized with the weakness of Stubb, the second mate. Stubb could be a character in a comedy of humors, his humor being jollity. He goes down to Davy Jones's locker, jesting, grinning at the grinning whale, reading Moby Dick, as Ahab does, in terms of his ruling passion. One of his sayings sums up his character: "A laugh's the wisest, easiest answer to all that's queer." But in a crisis a laugh evades the issue as much as sentimentalism does. Ahab condemns both Stubb and Starbuck with clarity and intensity. On the first day of the chase, the sight of Ahab's boat, wrecked and reversed—an omen certainly—drew a jest from Stubb and a warning from Starbuck. To Ahab jest and warning were alike expressions of mankind's fatal mediocrity, its submissiveness, its incapacity to rebel. Against that fatal mediocrity Ahab set his own equally fatal pride:

"Begone! Ye two are the opposite poles of one thing; Starbuck is Stubb reversed, and Stubb is Starbuck; and ye two are all mankind; and Ahab stands alone among the millions of the peopled earth, nor gods nor men his neighbors!"

What, then, of Ishmael? It must be remembered that he went to sea in order to meditate upon the world and the occupants thereof, including the white whale. He solved his problem day by day, responding with a poet's sensitivity to mood and character and situation and with a poet's disdain of logical consistency. If a pattern can be discovered in a bewildering variety of musings and meditations, it is one that might be thought of, in musical metaphor, as divisions upon a ground. The ground has been laid down by Solomon and Ecclesiastes. The theme is weariness and disillusion. All things are full of labor; man cannot utter it. It is wise to live sparely. Be like the whale, Ishmael advises, equalize your temperature. If an even balance proves difficult, lean to the sad side. But don't lean too far over. "There is a wisdom that is woe [Ecclesiastes'] but there is a woe that is madness [Ahab's]." Faith helps to maintain the balance. But it is a hard-won and earth-bound faith; it does not embrace the frame of things or extend to any Framer. Despite the fact that "in many of its aspects this visible world seems formed in love," the conclusion is that "the invisible spheres were formed in fright." And the gods themselves "are not for ever glad. The ineffaceable, sad birth-mark in the brow of man, is but the stamp of sorrow in the signers." This would seem to be the voice of the solemn ground.

But there are flights. Ishmael admires the souls that can soar like the Catskill eagle, and his own soul can take flight occasionally. Normally, it would seem, he believes in playing safe. He advises against pushing off into strange seas of thought. Having considered the cruelty of the sea, he turns with relief to "this green, gentle, and most docile earth." And he continues:

"For as this appalling ocean surrounds the verdant land, so in the soul of man there lies one insular Tahiti, full of peace and joy, but encompassed by all the horrors of the half known life. God keep thee! Push not off from that isle, thou canst never return!"

Yet he can grow lyrical over Bulkington, the spirit in man that makes him more adventurous than even the Catskill eagle:

But as in landlessness alone resides the highest truth, shoreless, indefinite as God—so, better is it to perish in that howling infinite, than be ingloriously dashed upon the lee, even if that were safety! For worm-like, then, oh! who would craven crawl to land! Terrors of the terrible! is all this agony so vain? Take heart, take heart, O Bulkington! Bear thee grimly, demigod! Up from the spray of thy ocean-perishing—straight up, leaps thy apotheosis!

He grows lyrical, again, over the dignity of man. Not always realized, it nevertheless abounds, and its source is in God himself: "His omnipresence, our divine equality!" Standing at the masthead, over the rolling ship and the rolling sea, he can enter into a cosmic consciousness, wherein the ship borrows its motion from the sea, and the sea borrows hers from "the inscrutable tides of God." But he fears these pantheistic moods and warns against them. He can pass into the very opposite mood, in times of extreme tribulation, and take "this whole universe for a vast practical joke." But wayward moods easily give way to faith and fellowship. The friendship of Queequeg is a restorative, or the feel of soft, sweet ambergris in the hand. Despite the solemn ground which is its natural home, Ishmael's soul takes wing at many a call. Of this dual character Ishmael is proud:

And so, through all the thick mists of the dim doubts in my mind, divine intuitions now and then shoot, enkindling my fog with a heavenly ray. And for this I thank God; for all have doubts; many deny; but doubts or denials, few along with them have intuitions. Doubts of all things earthly, and intuitions of some things heavenly; this combination makes neither believer nor infidel, but makes a man who regards them both with equal eye.

Character is fate, it has been said; and I hope that Ishmael's fate is implicit in his character. The essential thing about that character is its apparently limitless understanding and compassion. Ishmael lends his own identity to others, even to the point of having little or none himself. He pulls an oar in Queequeg's boat when boats are lowered, but he is seldom seen in this or any other physical activity. But spiritually he is everywhere and nowhere, observing and comprehending. In a dictator's way it is Ahab's crew; they jump when he commands. In a poet's way the crew is Ishmael's; they are his by assimilation. Not a man upon that ship but is understood and provisionally accepted, although several of them are eventually brought to judgment. It is the attitude of mind that an author may have toward the characters, good and bad, that he has created. It is the attitude of mind that a psychotherapist takes toward his patients. Its healing quality is discussed by Dr. Jung, who says:

This may sound like a scientific precept, and may be confused with a purely intellectual and detached attitude of mind. But what I mean to convey is something quite different. It is a human quality—a kind of deep respect for facts and events and for the person who suffers from them—a respect for the secret of such a human life. The truly religious person has this attitude. He knows that God has brought all sorts of strange and inconceivable things to pass, and seeks in the most curious ways to enter a man's heart. He therefore senses in everything the unseen presence of the divine will. This is what I mean by "unprejudiced objectivity." It is a moral achievement on the part of the doctor, who ought not to let himself be repelled by illness and corruption. We cannot change anything unless we accept it.

This provisional acceptance of all men is, as Dr. Jung says, a kind of religious faith. It is the kind of religious faith that Ishmael has, and the kind he shares with Queequeg. This is the bond that makes them brothers. The kinship is recognized by both of them from first to last, and particularly by Ishmael in the chapter entitled "The Monkey Rope." The hazards of whaling have on this occasion placed Queequeg "down there in the sea," where he stands unsteadily and perilously on the back of a captured whale, while Ishmael remains on deck trying to hold him safe by means of a rope fastened at one end to Queequeg's belt, at the other to his own. "So, then," Ishmael reflected, "an elongated Siamese ligature united us. Queequeg was my own inseparable twin brother." As Ishmael pondered over this physical relationship, he found it becoming—it is his own word— metaphysical. "I seemed distinctly to perceive that my own individuality was now merged in a joint stock company of two." The merger began the first day of their acquaintance, and not without formality. Immediately Ishmael felt the healing quality of this new friendship. "No more," he tells us, "my splintered heart and maddened hand were turned against the wolfish world. This soothing savage had redeemed it." Introducing Queequeg to Captain Bildad, Ishmael declared:

"He's a member of the first Congregational Church. . . . I mean, sir, the same ancient Catholic Church to which you and I, and Captain Peleg there, and Queequeg here, and all of us, and every mother's son and soul of us belong; the great and everlasting First Congregation of this whole worshipping world; we all belong to that."

Only a little while before, Queequeg had proved his membership. On the way from New Bedford to Nantucket he had leaped into dangerous waters to rescue a boy who had mocked him. Heroic? No, just in the line of duty. "It's a mutual, joint-stock world, in all meridians," he seemed to say. "We cannibals must help these Christians." This is the first step in the faith that saves. Queequeg held it in his noble savage way, Ishmael in his noble Presbyterian way. On the morning after their first night together, Ishmael awoke to find Queequeg's arm thrown round him. That arm was again thrown round him when he floated off to safety on Queequeg's life-buoy.

NOTES

Quotations from *Moby-Dick* are in conformity with the edition published by the Oxford University Press (1947) and edited by Willard Thorp. Permission has been kindly granted. This edition is a careful reprint of the first American edition. References are to pages, without statement of title.

Thanks are also due to the Princeton University Press for permission to quote from Kierkegaard's *Fear and Trembling, The Sickness unto Death,* and *The Concept of Dread;* to the Macmillan Company for permission to quote from A. E.'s "Krishna," from Martin Buber's *Between Man and Man,* and from the same author's *The Prophetic Faith;* to Harcourt, Brace and Company for permission to quote from C. G. Jung's *Modern Man in Search of a Soul;* to the Yale University Press for permission to quote from C. A. Bennett's *A Philosophical Study of Mysticism;* and to the Massachusetts Historical Society for permission to quote from *The Education of Henry Adams.*

PAGE

4 And if: p. 40.
   The ribs: p. 39.
   Kings: I Kings 16:30–33.

5 durst fix: *Paradise Lost,* I, 382–91.

6 the duality: the duality in King Ahab's mind is brought out in the following passage: "As Solomon set up a cult of the Sidonian Astarte for his Sidonian wife, so Ahab set up for his Tyrian wife a cult of the Tyrian Baal, ... the only difference being that, unlike Solomon, Ahab himself worshipped the foreign deity—even though he gave his sons names that testified to his worship of YHVH—and thereby betrayed his duty

PAGE

as the anointed of Israel's God" (Martin Buber, *The Prophetic Faith* [New York, 1949], p. 76).

insane earnestness: p. 88.

what's signed: p. 89.

7 cannibal of: p. 66.

a crucifixion, p. 115.

cut away: p. 114.

8 deep scars: *Paradise Lost*, I, 601–4.

restless thoughts: *Samson Agonistes*, ll. 19–22.

9 Not force: *Paradise Regained*, I, 97.

It drew: p. 150

the same: p. 152

10 some sort: p. 155

11 communion with: I Cor. 10:20.

13 No, no: p. 457.

But what's: p. 153.

Vengeance on: p. 153.

14 certain morbidness: p. 70. Kierkegaard agrees, quoting Seneca: "Nullum exstitit ingenium sine aliqua dementia" (see *Journals* [New York, 1938], Nos. 459, 1135, 673).

grand programme: p. 7.

dark recesses: p. 174.

PAGE

15 about that: p. 88.

His three: p. 172.

Ahab and: p. 173.

16 swung to: p. 173.

there are: Kierkegaard, *Journals, passim*, but esp. Nos. 1228, 825, 673.

Hadst thou: *The Golden Sayings of Epictetus* (London, 1909), No. cxli.

17 Who's over: p. 154.

never saw: p. 216.

Before Thee: *Journals*, No. 825.

18 His ivory: p. 434.

To be: *Journals*, No. 673.

then it: *Ibid.*, No. 825.

Richard III: *Ibid.*, No. 673; see also *Fear and Trembling* (Princeton, 1945), pp. 163 f.

19 All that: p. 173.

20 unearthly conceit: p. 170.

though groves: p. 171.

grand hooded: p. 8.

Aside from: p. 176.

21 at once: p. 183.

22 I heard: A. E. (G. W. Russell), "Krishna."

The sphere: Charles A. Bennett, *A Philosophical Study of Mysticism* (New Haven, 1923), p. 142.

A Reading of Moby-Dick

PAGE

The Poem of Job (London, 1947), p. 45.

88 The heart: Jer. 17:9.
a little: Jerusalem, p. 96, l. 28.
Wilt thou: Job 40:8.
the holiest: p. 177.

89 To neither: p. 471.

92 By whatsoever: Apuleius, The Golden Ass (trans. Adlington), Book xi.
I am: Ibid.

93 Verily at: Hesiod Theogony ("Loeb Classical Library"), p. 87.
Part of: Faust, I, 3 (trans. Bayard Taylor).

94 To me: Three Greek Plays, trans. Edith Hamilton (New York, 1937), p. 137.

96 Ha, ha: p. 479.

98 Hands off: p. 483.
He saw: p. 390.
Oh God: p. 483.

99 This boy: Coriolanus, V, 3.
There is: p. 493.

100 No, no: pp. 493–94.

101 Only when: Kierkegaard, The Concept of Dread (Princeton, 1946), p. 107.
If I: King John, IV, 1.

PAGE

102 Now, then: p. 489.
The things: p. 520.

103 Listen, and: p. 494.

104 Perhaps this: C. G. Jung, Modern Man in Search of a Soul (New York, 1933), p. 271.

106 Ha! yonder: p. 500.
even as: p. 495.

107 Here's food: p. 521.

108 a tear: William Blake, Jerusalem, p. 52.
Close! stand: p. 502.

110 Knowledge we: John Drinkwater, "A Prayer."
There she: p. 505.
So far: p. 489.

111 If we: The aphorism is John Smith's, the Cambridge Platonist (see F. J. Powicke, The Cambridge Platonists [London, 1926], p. 19).
He became: Four Zoas, Night IV, l. 285.

112 whence is: St. Augustine Confessions Book vii.
is that: Kierkegaard, Fear and Trembling, p. 64.
that wills: Kierkegaard, The Sickness unto Death, p. 118.